BEVERLY MASSACHUSETTS

ROCKPORT
PUBLISHERS

Logo Savvy

Top brand-design firms share their
naming and identity strategies

Perry Chua & Dann Ilicic ~ WOW Branding

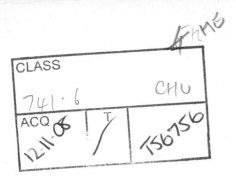
© 2007 by Rockport Publishers, Inc.
This paperback edition first published in 2008

First published in the United States of America by
Rockport Publishers, a member of
Quayside Publishing Group
100 Cummings Center
Suite 406-L
Beverly, Massachusetts 01915-6101
Telephone: (978) 282-9590
Fax: (978) 283-2742
www.rockpub.com

Library of Congress Cataloging-in-Publication Data
Logo savvy : top brand design firms share their naming and identity strategies
/ Wow Branding.
     p.   cm.
  ISBN 1-59253-304-3 (hardcover)
  1. Logos (Symbols)—Catalogs. 2. Corporate image—Catalogs. 3. Business
names—
 Catalogs. I. Wow Branding (Firm)
NC1002.L63L657 2007
741.6—dc22

2006026687
CIP

ISBN-13: 978-1-59253-507-1
ISBN-10: 1-59253-507-0

10 9 8 7 6 5 4 3 2 1

Design: WOW Branding
Design Team: Perry Chua, Will Johnson, Jeff Schramm
Project Manager: Karen West
Production Managers: Zoë MacKenzie, Angelo Cikes

Congratulations to the amazing talent from around the globe, as this book would not be what it is without your contribution.

We'd like to extend a special thank-you to Rockport Publishers for their patience, guidance, and sharing in our vision. And, of course, a big thank you to our families, both at home and at WOW, for their relentless support and dedication.

Contents

Introduction

Ever wonder how some of the world's top brand identity firms go about creating names and identity design for their clients? If you're as curious as we were, you'll find this book to be a tremendous resource. Every brand has a story and we've found the world's most unique approaches to bringing those stories to life.

This book is filled with over 300 examples from thirty two firms representing ten countries and six continents (nope, no entries from Antarctica). We've organized them by the seven naming categories we use at WOW Branding. Now, we're not saying these categories are necessarily the ones used by the participating firms, or even that our methods are the universal standard. The truth is, there's no school for naming—last we checked, you couldn't even get a degree in naming—but everyone seems to have an opinion on naming. The only way to truly test whether a name is any good is to keep an eye on it for years, maybe decades. But since none of us can wait that long, learning from those who make their living by creating names and brands seems to be the next best thing.

Over the years, we've developed a number of tools and techniques that help us with the naming process and now, for the first time ever, we're going to share them with you. You'll find tips for all three phases of naming: Strategic, Creative, and Legal. We're even including the actual worksheets we use for every naming project we do.

If you've ever yanked your hair out trying to come up with the perfect name—and who hasn't?—we sincerely hope the information presented here will help alleviate some of the frustration on your next project. One thing we know for certain is that when a trusted process is combined with a talented team, magic is bound to happen.

Clients seem to find comfort in knowing that a proven process exists. There is nothing more frightening to a client than believing we're all a bunch of creative junkies waiting for the next inspirational hallucination—although that's bound to happen, too. You'll build a lot of confidence with your clients by getting the strategic portion of the naming project just right—especially when it comes to identifying and establishing solid and well-articulated brand positioning.

Most clients will naturally gravitate towards descriptive names because they seem logical. Unfortunately—or fortunately, depending on your point of view—descriptive names are generally impossible to trademark. The best names tend to reflect a company's personality—based more on the "who," "how," and "why" of their business rather than the "what" and "where." Descriptions should be saved for taglines and positioning lines. Our Naming Evaluation Worksheet will help both you and your client assess the top name choices by taking their many attributes into consideration.

We'd like to extend our gratitude to all the firms that sent us projects for consideration. In total, we entertained over 500 entries, all of which merited inclusion. In the end—of a long and painful process—we selected the projects that provided the greatest variety of thinking, approach, and style.

Good luck and good process on your next naming project.

Perry Chua & Dann Ilicic
WOW Branding

Branding Is Not Marketing

Many people assume that branding is something that falls somewhere between the creative team and the marketing department. Our view at WOW is that branding is actually a CEO-level initiative that drives the entire organization—in fact, from our perspective, branding has very little to do with the marketing department at all.

There's a simple little formula we use to explain branding:

Design an authentic and differentiating Brand Promise

+

Align your company to be a Promise Delivery System (and nothing else)

———————————

Brand Success

A common question we get asked by prospective clients is, "How do we get the word out?" Our question back to them is, "So, what's the word?" What exactly is the compelling, authentic, and differentiating brand promise you want to get out? We have yet to meet a client who is able to answer this question with complete conviction. The good thing is that we have a process for extracting and revealing this and other key information—information we have found to be critical in developing a successful brand.

There are four primary areas we look at when beginning any branding project:

1. Do you know who you are?

2. Do you know how you are currently positioned in the marketplace and/or what your strategic positioning should be?

3. Does your brand identity reflect who you are and your positioning?

4. How will you communicate your brand—first to your employees and then to your customers?

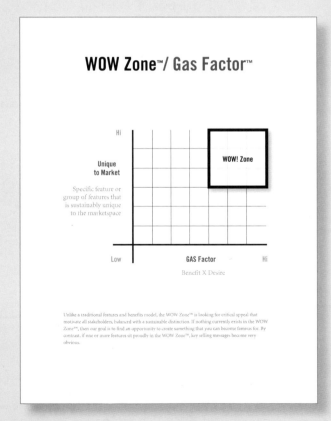

WOW Zone™/ Gas Factor™

Hi

Unique to Market

Specific feature or group of features that is sustainably unique to the marketspace

WOW! Zone

Low   **GAS Factor**   Hi

Benefit X Desire

Unlike a traditional features and benefits model, the WOW Zone™ is looking for critical appeal that motivate all stakeholders, balanced with a sustainable distinction. If nothing currently exists in the WOW Zone™, then our goal is to find an opportunity to create something that you can become famous for. By contrast, if one or more features sit proudly in the WOW Zone™, key selling messages become very obvious.

■ Welcome to the "WOW Zone™." The WOW Zone™ helps define your brand's position by demonstrating two things: why you're different and why you're better.

The first three areas define the core of the brand. This is often referred to as the brand essence, brand platform, or simply, the brand core. No matter what you want to call it, this will be the basis for everything your company will become.

The fourth area breaks off into two parts: operations and marketing. How your brand is communicated internally is just as important as how it will be communicated to your

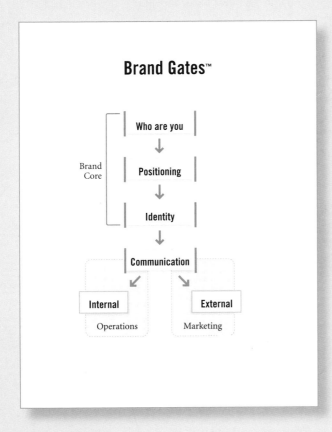

customers. Ultimately, every operational facet of the company must get intimately and obviously linked to the brand core—hiring, accounting, shipping, business development, etc. There is nothing more tragic for a company than when its insiders are clueless about the brand and their role in delivering the brand promise. At the very least, we advocate making sure that you share all new products, ads, promotions, and press releases with your employees before anyone else.

Finally, we come to the marketing department. Communicating to the target customer group becomes a lot easier once the brand core and promise have been clearly defined and the company has transformed itself into a promise delivery system. The marketers can now concentrate on defining their tactics and unleashing their creativity against that brand core.

DO YOU KNOW WHO YOU ARE?

Surprisingly, many clients do not have a clear, well-articulated understanding of who they are. Finding that out is our first step in the branding process. We need to extract the answers to the following questions:

1. What are the core values: what is important, what are your principles, what will govern your existence?

2. What is the core purpose of the organization: why does it exist, why is it meaningful? A great core purpose has the power to unite an organization.

3. What is the envisioned future or BHAG (that's Big, Hairy, Audacious Goal)? As part of this exercise, we like to have clients finish this sentence: "One day, we see a world where…" This is all about thinking big—really big—and looking twenty to twenty five years into the future. Here's a good test: If people complain that there is absolutely no way you can achieve your BHAG, they say it's the stupidest thing they've ever heard, or if they whisper behind your back that you've bought a one-way ticket to Crazytown, then you're definitely on the right track.

4. What are the short-, medium-, and long-term goals for the organization: what will it look like one year, five years, and ten years from now?

5. What is the business model: how do you make money, how will you measure economic performance and success?

Once you've got a grip on who you are and what you stand for, the next step in defining your brand strategy is determining how you are currently positioned versus how you should be positioned. Positioning is really all about figuring out how your company fits into the marketplace. Remember, it's what makes you different and what makes you better. In order to define this, we ask the following questions:

1. What do you want to be famous for? What's your promise: when people think of you, what words or thoughts will come to mind? This is usually where taglines, positioning lines, and mantras are useful—as long as they're not chock-full of marketing hyperbole. A simple core purpose and ambitiously envisioned future play a major role in defining your fame.

2. Do you know who your ideal customers are? What else do they buy; what are their likes and dislikes? It's also helpful to identify the customer that you don't want—many times this is much easier than defining your ideal customer. We talk to customers and, whenever possible, observe their behavior to gain insight into how they think about your category.

3. Who are your competitors? Who else does your customer consider when shopping your category and how do you compare to the other company? Is there a category leader? Will you look like you belong in the category or will you be dramatically different?

4. What is the buying process? Exactly what steps do your customers go through in order to make a purchase decision? How can you make that decision process easier?

5. Why should they buy from you? Are there clearly articulated and truthful sales messages that demonstrate why you're different and better? Can everyone in your company explain why customers should buy from you? (See page 8, WOW Zone™ diagram.)

6. Will you bear the risk of your promise? There's a saying we use in our office: "Who shall bear the risk of a promise—the promise maker or the promise taker?" We find there is no better way to promise authenticity than by assigning accountability.

7. What does your brand architecture look like? Defining the relationships between the company, its subsidiaries, and its product early on can save time, money, and, most importantly, headaches.

8. What are your primary and secondary brand touch points? Brand touch points are every possible interaction or experience someone will have with your brand. We like to break them up into three categories: prepurchase, purchase, and post-purchase. Every touch point matters: from how phones are answered to package design to how easy your product is to use.

9. What are your ten words? We've done away with the traditional creative brief because we've found that distilling our findings into ten evocative words is a much smarter way to translate a brand strategy (the combination of who you are plus your positioning) into a brand identity.

Names Are Made Great

There's no question that a great name is the keystone for a great brand identity. A name is a handle from which all the attributes of the brand will ultimately hang. More importantly, the name gives the brand an opportunity to be memorable, distinctive, ownable, and identifiable. To test this theory, simply imagine if people had no names—we'd all be reduced to long-winded descriptions and exhausting finger pointing to identify and understand each other.

We are often asked, "What makes a great name?" The truth is, that's the wrong question. The right question is, "What do we do to make the name great?" Think of it as building a reputation with which the name will be associated. Can you remember when you first heard of Yahoo!, Google, Kinko's, or Apple? Many people first deemed these company names immature, foolish, and inappropriate. Yet these company names prevailed because of what their companies put behind them: how they built their brand identity and what they came to represent.

The best names capture the essence of the organization—and, yes, there is a process for finding that essence. We approach naming in three distinct stages: Strategic, Creative, and Legal.

START WITH STRATEGY

Developing and understanding strategy is essential. It's like coming up with a title for a book—it's a hell of a lot easier if you know the story. Creating a company story is one of the first things we do in the naming process. For us, this means spending time with the visionaries—usually the CEO—to get a deep understanding of the core purpose of the organization. Oftentimes, this also means defining the true core purpose itself. To further understand the client's business, we then do a

Naming Worksheet™

The name will be one of the most identifiable elements for the entire life of the brand. Creating the right name is a mix of creativity, meaning, impact, use and of course, availability. WOW's naming process starts by exploring possibilities in each of the following categories. As you work through this sheet, you may find that some names are actually a combination of more than one. The goal of this exercise is to get as many ideas as possible and uncover which stream the greatest. For this reason we ask that you contribute a minimum of four options within each category.

Playful >>	
Origin >>	
Invented >>	
Descriptive >>	
Technical >>	
Conjoined >>	
Acronym >>	
Metaphoric >>	
Random >>	

Playful, Irreverent, Arbitrary, Oxymoron
Names that challenge the ordinary.
(Yahoo / Monster / Steel Magnolia's / Guess?)

Origin, Founder, Location, Cultural Bias
Names that pay tribute to a specific inspiration or contribution to birth of the brand. (Eddie Bauer / Ford / Hilton / Rolls Royce / Chevrolet / North Face / IKEA)

Invented
Completely made up words. (Kodak / Viagra)

Descriptive/Association
Deliberately clear descriptions or attribute.
(Volkswagen / Caterpillar / Bed Bath & Beyond / Holiday Inn / Kitchen Aid / Bell)

Technical
Names that blend a mix of modern words, technical language and specific function.
(Panasonic, Xerox)

Conjoined
Names that are a combination or connection of two or more ideas. (Fed Ex / Microsoft / Bisquick)

Acronym, Abbreviation
Names that stated as a group of letters that are intended to become the common name.
(BMW / IBM / BBC / UPS)

Metaphorical, Attribute, Analogy, Symbolism
Names that borrow from stories, cultural icons, or other emotive forces. (Apple / Mustang / Virgin / Monster / Starbucks)

Random Words, Appropriation
Completely random words that will be appropriate for the new concept over time. (Old Navy /Section 3)

■ Great ideas can be plucked from the oddest of places, and that's why the naming process at WOW is always a collaborative process. Like ingredients in a recipe, we gather our best creative thinkers and use our Naming Worksheet™ to help stir the batter. The concept of this exercise is: the more ideas, the better. Plus, by developing names in all nine categories, we'll make sure all the bases are covered. Go to www.wowbranding.com/namingworksheet to download a PDF of this worksheet.

In every single case, the name that ends up winning is the name with the best story—the name that can inspire a constant stream of solid ideas.

Naming Criteria Evaluation Sheet™

On a scale of 1 – 10, rank the names individually. This is not a comparison exercise.
All names can be strong and weak in various categories.

Name Selection	NAME#1	NAME#2	NAME#3	NAME#4	NAME#5
Is your first impression of the name strong?					
Does it sound/look good?					
Is it easy to read/pronounce?					
Use it in multiple sentences. Does it feel right?					
Are quick associations positive? Does it have story appeal?					
Does it relate to the primary benefit(s) of the company/service?					
Does it sound credible?					
Can it work internationally?					
Does it have verb or generic potential?					
Is it memorable?					
How nervous does it make you?					
How well does it relate to your positioning or who you are?					
Total Score					

10-WORD CREATIVE BRIEF

》
》
》
》
》
》
》
》
》
》

■ All names must pass WOW's rigorous ten-point Naming Criteria test. Try it with your own company's name and see how it measures up. Go to www.wowbranding.com/namingcriteria to download this PDF.

competitive analysis to get a complete picture of the industry from a customer perspective. The deeper you dig, the better the story. (See page 9, Brand Gates™.)

GENERATE CONCEPTS

The creative is both the fun and tedious part of the naming process. It is not uncommon for us to generate thousands of names for a project—which can make selecting a single name the most daunting task of all. To aid this process, we challenge our staff to develop a story for every name that makes the short list. The story is usually built on, and inspired by, the events, scenarios, and messages that are associated with the name. In every single case, the name that ends up winning is the name with the best story—the name that can inspire a constant stream of solid ideas. We've included a few samples of the worksheets we use to help generate names across a number of categories.

MAKE SURE YOU CAN USE IT

The legal search for trademark availability is the dreaded part of any naming process. How many times have we fallen blissfully in love with a name that belongs to another? Our hearts have been broken far too often to count. When our trademark attorney approaches us with the unhappy news, we have to re-evaluate our plan. Sometimes, it means going with our second-favorite choice. Sometimes, it means starting from scratch. Presenting names to a client always involves incorporating certain visual elements of their identity to help tell the stories behind them. Our goal is to get them to fall in love. Once we've presented, we ask them to reserve all judgment until they have lived with the new name for at least three days. That means the client can "try on" the name: introducing themselves with the new moniker, adding it to their phone greeting, assessing exactly how it makes them feel. By putting it to work, the new name truly comes to life.

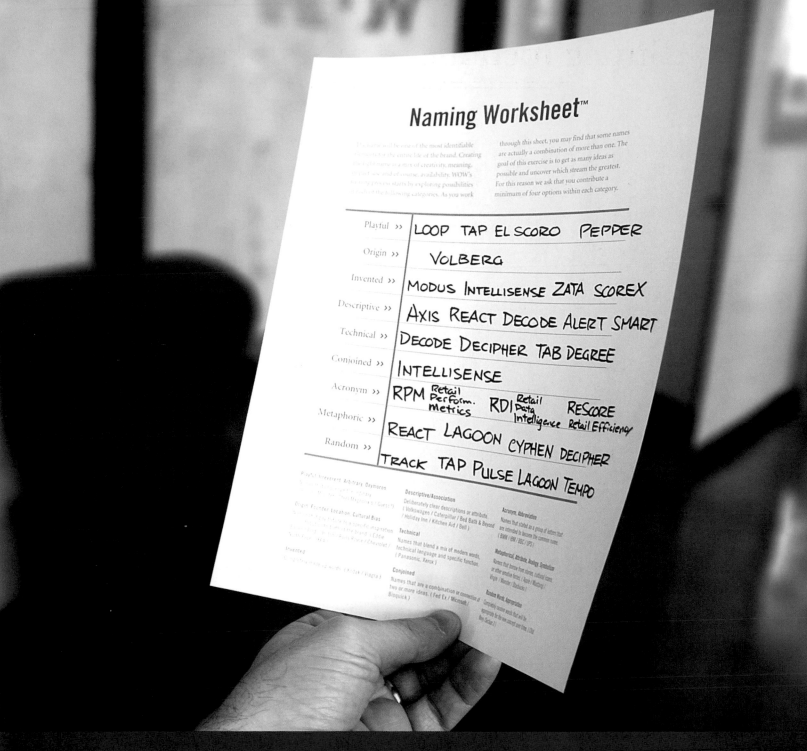

The best names capture the essence of the organization—
and yes, there is a process for finding that essence.

Strong Identities Are Authentic

WHO ARE YOU?

Before we design a logo or corporate identity, there are a few things we need to know about the brand's personality. Defining a personality is the first step to creating a strong and meaningful brand identity.

To do this, we look at things such as the company's vision and values and where they fit into customers' perspective and the competitive landscape. Your brand identity can be defined as the expression of who you really are and how you're strategically positioned in the marketplace. We highlight three important steps in our comprehensive naming and brand identity process.

WOW IF YOU WERE A…™

The "WOW If you were a…™" exercise uses social, visual, and nonvisual cues to help define the brand. Assigning personality characteristics to your brand will help you and your consumers establish emotional and cultural references for it. We've found that when we ask ourselves to choose a vehicle or celebrity to represent a brand, it begins to develop a very specific, distinct personality. Meryl Streep driving a yellow Beetle convertible through dusty country roads in the south of France paints a vivid picture—a great springboard for the designer's creative process. We can examine the reasons why Meryl Streep was chosen; established, mature, and respected come to mind. The yellow Beetle was selected because of its quirky, free-spirited qualities; the fact that it's a convertible means fun. By combining these descriptive words together, we now have some key attributes of the brand.

WOW ATTRIBUTE SPECTRUM™

Like the previous exercise, the "WOW Attribute Spectrum™" helps us define some key visual and character traits to express

Attribute Spectrum™

Necessity ››	‹‹ Luxury
Expensive ››	‹‹ Economical
Light ››	‹‹ Serious
Formal ››	‹‹ Casual
Exotic ››	‹‹ Commonplace
Discreet ››	‹‹ Aggressive
Hi-Tech Industrial ››	‹‹ Homemade
Heritage ››	‹‹ Ground Breaking
Modern ››	‹‹ Classic
Quiet ››	‹‹ Loud
Simple ››	‹‹ Complex
Subdued ››	‹‹ Bright
Black & White ››	‹‹ Colourful
Feminine ››	‹‹ Masculine
Raw ››	‹‹ Refined

■ The "sliders" in the WOW Attribute Spectrum™ play an important role in establishing the brand's personality and character traits.

the brand. If we ask ourselves what the identity should look like, we can use the Attribute Spectrum to help us determine its personality. For example, we would discuss and agree upon whether the brand is timeless vs. modern, discreet vs. aggressive, subdued vs. colorful, etc. How do we want the brand to come across? What tone do we want the brand to have? What do we want to convey to the target audience?

WOW IDENTITY FUNNEL™

When we approach ideas for brand identity, we start by looking at the big picture. Some companies may start the project by incorporating design elements into a logo and then later applying them across the entire identity system. We prefer to approach it the other way—to explore ideas and concepts around color stories, photography/illustration style,

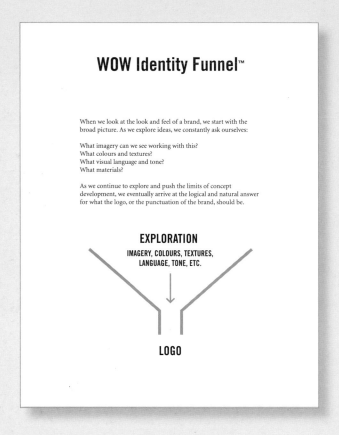

By applying the WOW Identity Funnel™ way of thinking, designers avoid developing identity systems around a logo. Instead, they focus on the brand touch points that matter most, to create memorable experiences at every level.

business card materials and shapes, brochure cover textures, brand behavior, etc. We ask ourselves, "What does it feel like to interact with the brand, from each touch point? What is the desired response when someone receives a business card?" As we continue to explore and push the limits of concept development, we eventually arrive at the logical and natural answer for what the logo should be. For example, a brand

identity with a bright, energetic color story and bold photography might warrant an elegant "wordmark" as its logo. (A wordmark is a standardized graphic representation of the name of a company or product that is easily identifiable.) After all, a logo is simply the punctuation to a brand.

BEFORE PENCIL HITS PAPER

We must determine what the creative team needs to know before we begin the design process. After the first two "gates" (defining who you are and how you are positioned) have been successfully completed (See page 9, Brand Gates™), the rest of the creative brief will practically write itself.

In the positioning gate, we create something called a brand wall, which essentially provides us with the competitive landscape. We want to see what the customer sees. What are they looking at when they are faced with a decision? As brand designers, we have the ability to influence this decision through the power of a well-articulated messaging and design system. In assembling the brand wall, we try to gather as much relevant information as we can. From website home pages to literally "buying the shelf" at the supermarket, we can analyze the category by observing color dominance, graphical style, and positioning lines.

RESISTING TEMPTATION

Just as the world had decided to accept personal computers as boring beige boxes whose primary role was to perform mundane tasks, Apple surprised us with the iMac, a revolutionary machine bursting with personality. It was available in an assortment of funky colors (or fruit flavors, as they named them) to match its equally funky product design. Innovative design has always been a core value for the Apple team, and this key differentiation is evident in its positioning strategy.

Branding is about creating focus and clarity. Learn from Apple: take a risk, bite off more than you can chew, but resist the temptation of trying to be all things to all people.

POLISH THE IDEA, THEN THE WORK

Be sure to post your ten-point creative brief—your brand's key attributes—prominently in every brainstorming session. For

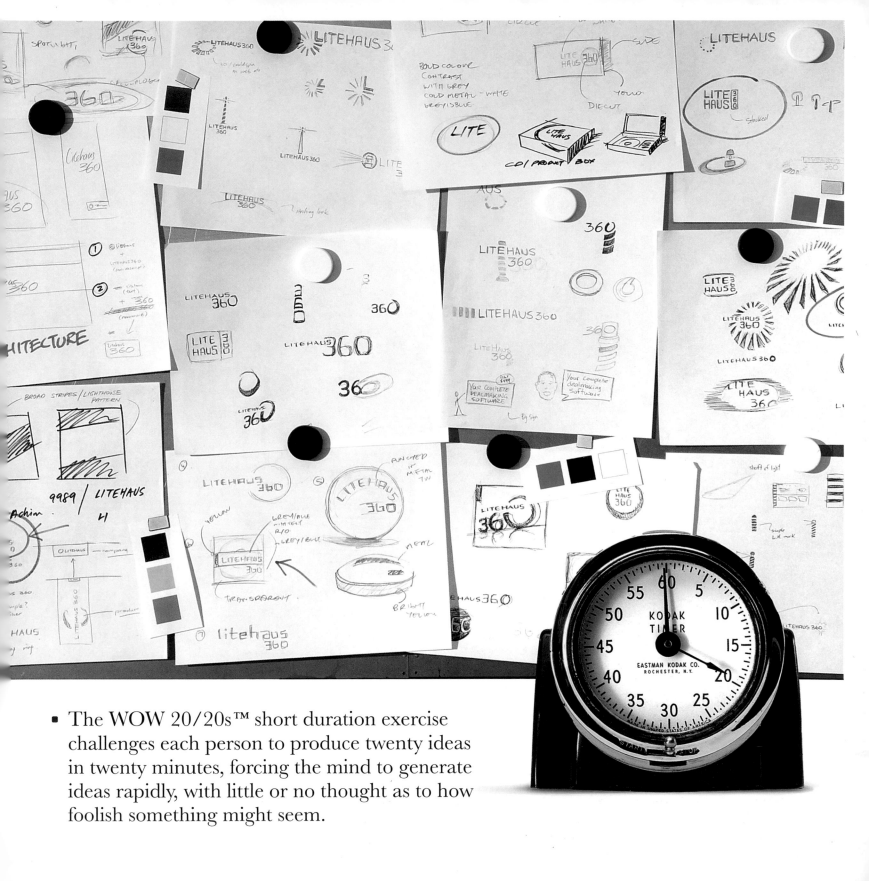

• The WOW 20/20s™ short duration exercise challenges each person to produce twenty ideas in twenty minutes, forcing the mind to generate ideas rapidly, with little or no thought as to how foolish something might seem.

the most effective brainstorming environment, we've created the "WOW 20/20™", where each person is charged with producing 20 different ideas in 20 minutes.

During the WOW 20/20™, team members are encouraged to push ideas beyond logo concepts, exploring elements of typographic style, photography/color relationship, textures, and three-dimensional forms. But the real beauty of this exercise lies within the twenty minute limit. The short duration forces the mind to generate ideas rapidly, with little or no time to edit thoughts for appropriateness. It also creates an environment without fear of uttering something that may be deemed ridiculous by others. Great ideas emerge from unexpected places. The best ones are built upon the single most outrageous thought that's so far out of left field it's not even in the ballpark—all because someone was brave enough to shout it out in front of everyone else.

EVALUATING THE IDEAS

As sketches are spread on the table, the group discusses the strengths and merits of each concept. The focus is always on the potential of the idea rather than its weakness. At this stage, it's important to remember that the goal of the 20/20™ is to generate as many ideas as possible. We're not only interested in the ideas but also where these ideas may take us—sometimes a friendly argument over the value of an idea may be the best way to test its validity or its ability to translate across a variety of media.

The best ideas should be chosen for their innovation, relevance, and pure passion. But keep in mind that the most innovative ideas might not be accepted right away. If it has never been seen or done before, it might make you feel uncomfortable—which is good! If your new identity doesn't make you nervous, even in the slightest, it's probably not creating the differentiation you need.

Creative vision is a subjective thing. What seems ridiculous to one designer may seem like the perfect solution to another. Designers should fight tirelessly for their concepts, refusing the alternatives, despite strong concerns from others in the group. We welcome and encourage an environment where such interaction can take place. Ultimately, it's the visionary's duty to express how the best idea fits the thought process and sell the idea to everyone else.

CAPTURING THE ESSENCE

A great deal of time should be dedicated to developing the one idea that captures the essence of the brand. We may go through dozens of WOW 20/20s™ until we feel we have gathered enough ideas in as many different directions as possible. As we move into brand implementation, this central concept, along with the ten-point creative brief, acts as a checkpoint throughout the entire creative process for how the brand should look, feel, and behave.

Creating a successful brand identity doesn't have to be complicated—stay focused, have fun along the way, and keep your process simple. Create an authentic and compelling promise and make sure your company is structured to consistently deliver on that promise.

Creative brainstorming can be an intense discipline, but don't forget to include healthy distractions from time to time. There is no formula for evaluating ideas. It usually comes down to a combination of relevance, degree of innovation, and the designer's passion.

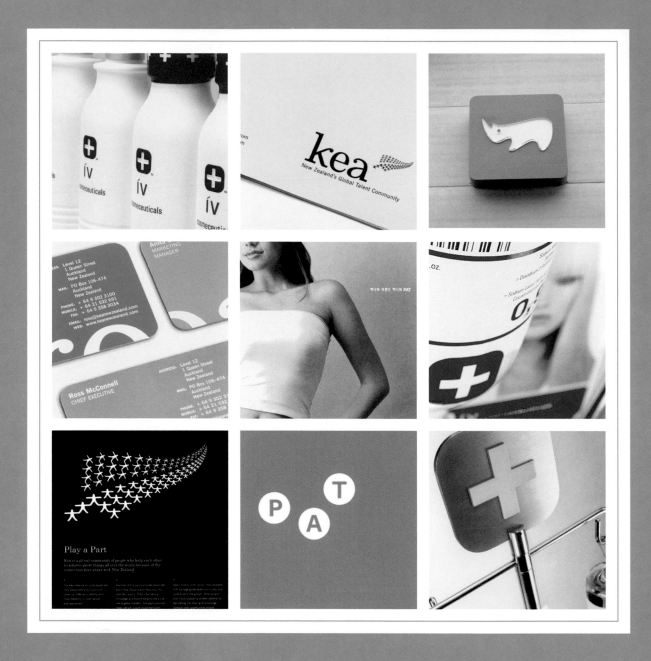

Acronym

Companies with long names tend to take advantage of
the brevity of an acronym. In many cases, the company
doesn't decide to adopt the acronym but customers
start using the acronym for ease and convenience.
Classic examples include International Business
Machines (IBM) and United Parcel Service (UPS).

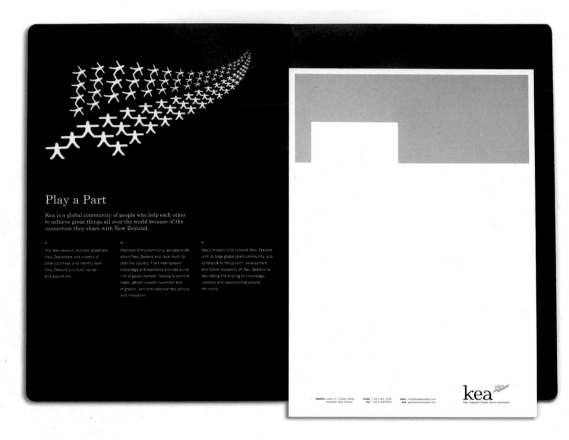

Play a Part

Kea is a global community of people who help each other to achieve great things all over the world because of the connection they share with New Zealand.

The Kea network includes expatriate New Zealanders and citizens of other countries who identify with New Zealand's culture, values and aspirations.

Members of this community are passionate about New Zealand and have much to offer the country. Their international knowledge and experience provides a vital link to global markets – helping to promote trade, attract inward investment and migration, and stimulate business activity and innovation.

Kea's mission is to connect New Zealand with its large global talent community, and contribute to the growth, development and future prosperity of New Zealand by facilitating the sharing of knowledge, contacts and opportunities around the world.

kea

■ For the primary color for the Kiwi Expat Assocation's (KEA) identity, Brave New World's (BNW) designers chose black because of its symbolic link to New Zealand. The secondary palette includes various hues that relate to the forest, farmland, sea, and sky. These warm and friendly shades communicate the organization's mission and enliven the primary color.

A COOPERATIVE STRATEGY

The Kiwi Expat Association (KEA) was founded with the goal of forging a relationship between New Zealand and its large expatriate workforce that is spread around the world. Today, KEA is a global community of people who are linked by their common passion for New Zealand, connecting more than 15,000 Kiwis and other friends of New Zealand in approximately 150 countries. In an effort to entice more New Zealanders to join this community, the KEA team engaged the Brave New World (BNW) design agency to make their brand more inspiring, contemporary, and credible.

Since its inception, members have shortened the name Kiwi Expat Association to KEA—an acronym that just happens to be the name of a native New Zealand mountain parrot known for its highly social and inquisitive nature. To build on the momentum that KEA had established locally and overseas, BNW kept the name but turned KEA into "Kea," making it friendlier and more approachable. They dropped Kiwi Expat Association and introduced the tagline, "New Zealand's global talent community." This positioning statement extends Kea's appeal beyond the traditional Kiwi expat and includes stakeholders inside and outside of New Zealand, since both are important to the long-term success of the organization.

DESIGN FIRM
BRAVE NEW WORLD

CREATIVE DIRECTOR
DEBBIE HYDE

DESIGNER
LUKE PITTAR

CLIENT
ROSS McCONNELL

The KEA wordmark is complemented by a fern, which is a well-known symbol of New Zealand, and is made up of "star people," a visual BNW created to represent the idea of connecting with others.

MAKING ITS MARK

The friendly wordmark, Kea, influenced by New Zealand's history and heritage, expresses how strongly New Zealanders are connected to their land. The Kea wordmark is complemented by a fern, which is a well-known symbol of New Zealand, and is made up of "star people," a visual BNW created to represent the idea of connecting with others. The combination of a national symbol with human figures conveys Kea's proud New Zealand heritage, the organization's dedication to supporting New Zealand interests around the world, and the fact that people will always be the most valuable part of Kea. To complement the illustration, BNW chose the Century typeface because it bridges the gap between friendly and formal.

BRINGING IT ALL TOGETHER

The new logo, color palette, and visual system convey confidence, communicate the importance of community, and express an inherent New Zealand spirit. Black was chosen as the primary shade—chosen because of its symbolic link to New Zealand. The secondary palette includes hearty New Zealand colors that relate to the forest, farmland, sea, and sky. These colors express a warm, friendly feel and offset the starkness of black and white. Kea's bold new logo is both beautiful and symbolic, important factors for any identity.

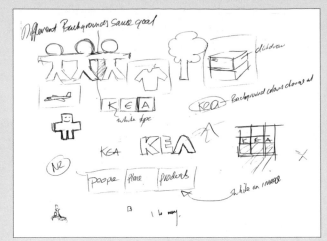

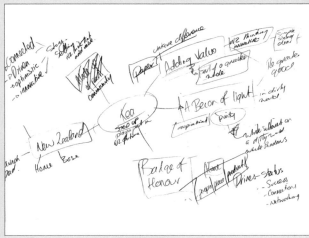

■ The key elements for the new identity for Kea, an organization dedicated to uniting New Zealanders around the world, was New Zealanders' connection to their land.

PHONE: + 64 9 302 3100
FAX: + 64 9 358 3034

EMAIL: info@keanewzealand.com
WEB: www.keanewzealand.com

ADDRESS: Level 12
1 Queen Street
Auckland
New Zealand

MAIL: PO Box 106-474
Auckland
New Zealand

PHONE: + 64 9 302 3100
MOBILE: + 64 21 532 691
FAX: + 64 9 358 3034

EMAIL: ross@keanewzealand.com
WEB: www.keanewzealand.com

McConnell
EXECUTIVE

Anita Boundy
MARKETING
MANAGER

Ross McConnell
CHIEF EXECUTIVE

ADDRESS: Level 12
1 Queen Street
Auckland
New Zealand

MAIL: PO Box 106-47
Auckland
New Zealand

PHONE: + 64 9 302
MOBILE: + 64 21 5
FAX: + 64 9 3

EMAIL: ross@ke
WEB: www.ke

• BNW chose the Century typeface because it bridges the
gap between friendly and formal.

A CLEAN START

Dossier was charged with creating a hair care brand sure to generate genuine excitement in an industry continually bombarded with flighty fashion trends. The brand's unique promise? These products would clean and shape hair as well as heal and revitalize damaged hair. Dossier transformed the products' simple attributes into an emotionally engaging brand that conveyed product efficacy and stylish elegance.

USING THEIR HEADS

Brainstorming concepts related to healing gave Dossier the appropriate inspiration for both the name and the look of the new product line. They explored the the medical field, a profession full of abbreviations and acronyms. One acronym with great potential was IV, which Dossier reappropriated to mean "Intense Vitalization," linking the name directly to the products' key attribute. The new name was paired with the word "cosmeceuticals," an emerging category that best describes this new product line and describes one that merges cosmetics and pharmaceuticals.

GETTING THE LOOK

The identity needed to express the products' dynamic balance between aesthetics and efficacy, snagging the attention of customers, yet delivering on the brand's promise. A recognizable cross icon efficiently communicated healing, but the challenge was how to combine that very traditional symbol with a sense of style. Using a restricted but evocative palette of red, white, and gray in an understated design approach, Dossier targeted the sweet spot between visually attractive and clinically effective. The packaging was built on a look and feel that accentuated the hip factor and an unusual bottle shape customized with a cartouche of the icon increased the bottle's tactile sensuality. Details like the tamperproof-style seal further supported the visual vocabulary.

▪ Using medical imagery and a limited color palette, Dossier targeted IV Cosmeceuticals' sweet spot— between visually attractive and clinically effective.

DESIGN FIRM
DOSSIER CREATIVE, INC.

CREATIVE DIRECTOR
DON CHISOLM

DESIGNERS
EENA KIM, DON CLELAND

CLIENT
IV COSMECEUTICALS

- Using an actual IV (intravenous) system as inspiration, point-of-purchase displays resembled modified IV stands topped by brushed aluminum versions of the icon. Other promotional pieces such as sales kits played off the concepts of first aid and emergency equipment.

- One acronym with great potential was IV, which Dossier reappropriated to mean "Intense Vitalization," linking the name directly to the products' key attribute. The new name was paired with the word "cosmeceuticals," an emerging category that best describes this new product line—one that merges cosmetics and pharmaceuticals.

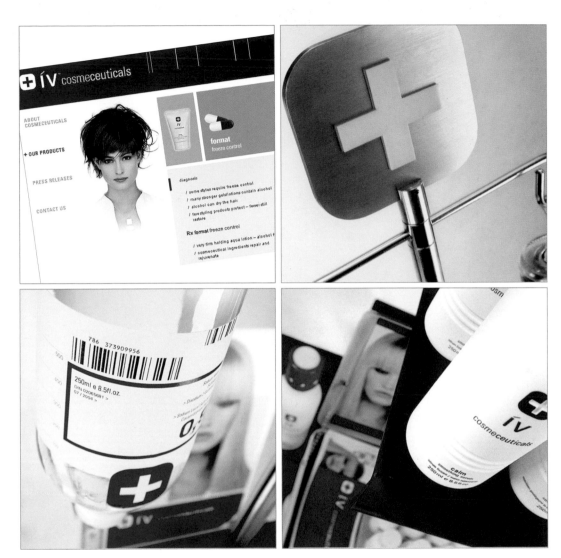

■ The strength of the IV Cosmeceuticals campaign comes down to its attention to details and consistency across all the materials. By playing off the idea of actual IV (intravenous) stands, the designers were able to push the concept to a truly memorable level.

APPLY, REPEAT

Using an actual IV system as inspiration, point-of-purchase displays resembled modified IV stands topped by brushed aluminum versions of the icon. When placed in high-end salons, these stands made a striking display in comparision to the other products on sale. Other promotional pieces such as sales kits played off the concepts of first aid and emergency equipment.

Keeping the brand focused on a specific visual language helped to create a consistent presentation in all expressions of the brand, from packaging to collateral and beyond. The result was just what the doctor ordered.

STYLISH ASPIRATIONS

PAT is a South Korean fashion merchandiser with over forty years experience in Asia. It distributes to more than 170 stores in South Korea alone and is increasing its presence in China with more than thirty stores built in major commercial cities such as Shanghai, Beijing, Tianjin, Dalian, and Guangzhou. The name PAT is an abbreviation of the corporate name, Pyung Ahn Textile.

When FutureBrand Japan was approached about this project, PAT's company image was that of an established, but outdated, fashion retailer that catered to the thirty-five plus market. The goal was to strengthen the brand's relevance with a modern, customer-friendly look and to broaden its consumer base without losing loyal shoppers.

PAT'S PERSONALITY

FutureBrand repositioned PAT as a trend leader with a happening attitude. The creatives defined personality attributes that would build a foundation for the brand's position in the marketplace—surprising, inspirational, modern, informal, inventive, confident, and passionate. The word fresh became the driving force behind the visual language, and FutureBrand condensed the theme into five short statements:

- A brand that projects your moods and inspires your mode
- Design that creates a light mood-elevating spirit
- A world of colors that unlocks casual elegance
- Service reflects the person you are
- Modern design, light and unforced

A BRAND NEW BRAND

The creatives wanted to break away from the current GAP look; to redefine PAT; and build PAT into a master brand, using the new brand design as a leitmotif for other sub-brands of the company to follow. To reposition the brand,

▪ A new brand has dramatically altered PAT's perception in the marketplace, making them a leader in the world of South Korean fashion.

FutureBrand focused on the three main areas that would best communicate the new direction of the company: identity, colors, and photography.

The existing identity, the rhino, was revamped in an illustrated style, transforming a literal image of the animal into a more modern, young, approachable and friendly brand icon. The modernized rhino shape was to become the hero of PAT,

DESIGN FIRM
FUTUREBRAND

CREATIVE DIRECTOR
WILLIAM WODUSCHEGG

DESIGNERS
MARTIN BROWN, RIVAKO TAKAHASHI

CLIENT
PAT

- After forty years, this established fashion retailer had become outdated. The goal of rebranding was to strengthen the brand's relevance with a modern, customer-friendly look to broaden its consumer base without losing loyal shoppers.

하나의 브랜드 하나의 **PAT**

이제 여러분들은 PAT브랜드의 힘 - 신선하고, 열려있는 태도를 보다 더 잘 이해할 것 입니다. 이제 여러분들이 무엇을 하든지, 어디에 있든지 간에 PAT브랜드를 향상시키 는데 그리고 가장 중요하게는 저희 고객들에게 PAT약속을 이행하는데 무엇을 해야 되는지 알 것입니다.

- The black-and-white photography creates an elegant look, complementing the color palette. A style guide dictated the proper combination of photography and color scheme to ensure consistency of the brand image.

 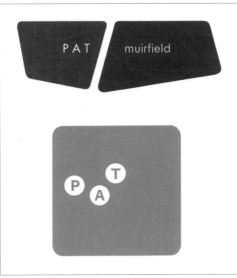 

■ The existing identity, the rhino, was revamped in an illustrated style, transforming
a literal image of the animal into an approachable and friendly brand icon.

moving the company towards its next stage of development. The new icon would influence the look and feel through all applications, and the goal was to build an emotional connection with the target audience, using the icon as part of brand's identity. The new, hip rhino helped drive the style of the photography, advertising, and even PAT's new collection.

The black-and-white photography created an elegant look, complementing the color palette. A style guide dictated the proper combination of photography and color scheme to ensure consistency of the brand image.

With its new identity, PAT managed to target a younger audience, increasing revenues in its new flagship stores. Since the launch of the new brand, its perception in the marketplace has drastically changed. The brand is now seen as exciting, evolving, and a leader in the world of fashion.

Conjoined

Names that combine or connect two or more words/memes
to create a new word are deemed to be conjoined. Technically,
conjoined names are invented, but their distinction lies in
the inherent familiarity in the words that make up the name.
Famous examples include TransAmerica and Microsoft.

:: Bloodorange

TASTING BLOODORANGE

Bloodorange is a clothing boutique in Sydney's Elizabeth Bay. It aims to be the first stop for fashion insiders looking for women's clothing by both international designers and homegrown talent. Layfield was commissioned to come up with a name, brand identity, and packaging for their store.

Creative director Stephen Layfield was determined to make Bloodorange stand out in the crowded fashion marketplace. The name was a huge advantage—it was edgy, distinctive, instantly memorable, and had visual potential. Research also showed that the name conjured up the right associations: premium, exclusive, and different.

A SWEET IDENTITY

The design concept plays on the contrasting properties of a blood orange, echoing the textured orange skin on the outside and the sensual ruby-red flesh inside. As a tasteful accent, Layfield's designers created a unique ribbon that acts as the signature for all Bloodorange brand packaging. Orange ribbon is printed with the white Bloodorange logotype on one side and is stitched with red satin ribbon on the reverse. As the ribbons are untied from the packaging, the luscious ruby-red color is revealed. This concept was also used for their folded business cards, which are printed matte orange on one side and open to reveal a high-gloss varnished red on the inside.

Simple in concept but rich and memorable in execution, this two-color theme plays across the retailer's signage, interiors, and packaging, leaving customers imagining a very sweet and somewhat exotic taste.

■ The overall design theme for the Bloodorange fashion store plays off the idea of a blood orange's color, textured skin, and luscious, juicy, red interior. Folded business cards are printed matte orange on the outside and open to reveal a high-gloss varnished red on the inside.

■ The designers at Layfield continued the theme across all of the retailer's marketing and merchandising materials and designed a unique ribbon that acts as the signature for all Bloodorange brand packaging. An orange ribbon is printed with the white Bloodorange logotype on one side and is stitched with red satin ribbon on the reverse.

DESIGN FIRM
LAYFIELD

CREATIVE DIRECTOR
STEPHEN LAYFIELD

DESIGNER
STEPHEN LAYFIELD

CLIENT
BLOODORANGE

Simple in concept but rich and memorable in execution, this two-color theme plays across the store's signage, interiors, and packaging, leaving customers imagining a very sweet and somewhat exotic taste.

:: Delisio

■ Brave New World's designers knew a fresh, hand-rendered typeface would best represent the personality of Delisio's potato chips. They sketched various versions to get the look and feel exactly right, then appointed an illustrator to craft each letter of the name.

SNACK STRATEGY

Bluebird Foods, the market leader of snack foods in New Zealand, engaged Brave New World (BNW) to name and package a potato chip brand that would appeal to adventurous yet discerning snackers—a segment of the snack market that wasn't addressed by any other potato chip brand. The name and, in turn, the packaging had to convey New Zealand's definition of the ultimate snack experience: the deli. Gourmet, unique, tempting, traditional, quality, and delicious became the key words as they concentrated on deli-sounding names.

The name they initially researched was Deliso, an evocative sound that they especially liked because it contained the word deli. Then an interesting thing happened; people in various focus groups automatically added an extra I to the third syllable, turning "Deliso" into "Delisio"—a fluid word that sounds Italian and even more like "delicious."

So Delisio it was. To communicate the deli environment with a slightly European feel, BNW designed a logo that's expressive, lively, and energetic. The designers knew a fresh, hand-rendered typeface would best represent Delisio's personality, resembling

the chalkboard menus of a real deli. Various versions were sketched to get the look and feel exactly right, then an illustrator was appointed to craft each letter of the name.

A color system—blue for sea salt, green for Greek tzatziki, rich red for sundried tomato and Parma ham, purple for feta cheese and roasted garlic—was introduced to differentiate the various chip flavors. The colors give Delisio chips a strong presence on the supermarket shelf and, at the same time, add sophistication to the brand that contrasts with the garish colors of most chip packaging.

The name Delisio, the thoughtful typography, the appetizing color palette, the beautiful food photography, the engaging story on the back of each package, and the use of matte foil packaging work together to put Delisio in an entirely different category than the shiny foil potato chip brands they compete with. This is the brand for people who enjoy new experiences and new tastes that transport them to a different location every time they open a bag, but it is the sales figures that have proved Delisio to be the chip that discerning consumers are proud to take home to their cupboards.

DESIGN FIRM
BRAVE NEW WORLD

CREATIVE DIRECTOR
DEBBIE HYDE

DESIGNER
ALI IRONS

CLIENT
BLUEBIRD FOODS

- Bluebird Foods, the market leader of snack foods in New Zealand, engaged Brave New World (BNW) to name and package a potato chip brand that would appeal to adventurous yet discerning snackers—a segment of the snack market that wasn't addressed by any other potato chip brand.

■ The intersecting V's of the newly designed Vancity logo express the concept of the bank often "being at the intersection" of pivotal moments in their members' lives. The color system has been designed to represent the three aspects of the credit union's business—personal banking (red), business banking (blue), and community (green).

LENDING VALUE

Vancity is Canada's largest credit union. Formed in 1945, they currently have more than 315,000 members and 42 branches throughout Greater Vancouver, the Fraser Valley, and Victoria. Vancity and its subsidiary companies are guided by a commitment to improve the quality of life in the communities where they live and work. Fueled by a desire to increase membership and better articulate its brand values, the original assignment for Karacters was to redesign the company's logo, then implement the new identity, "like for like," across all their materials.

A DIFFERENT KIND OF BANK

The initial research stage included a brand identity overview of the major local credit unions and banks, which revealed a somewhat homogeneous category. This presented Vancity an opportunity to differentiate itself from its competitors and a chance to truly innovate within its category.

Explorations began by drawing inspiration from a rich brand story developed prior to Karacters' involvement. The Vancity story identified the brand's personality as forward thinking, friendly, trusting, real, optimistic, and community oriented.

DESIGN FIRM
KARACTERS DESIGN GROUP

CREATIVE DIRECTOR
JAMES BATEMAN

DESIGNERS
MONICA MARTINEZ, KARA BOHL

CLIENT
VANCITY SAVINGS CREDIT UNION

A signage system dramatically elevated Vancity's street presence and allowed them to take ownership of the highly visible locations they occupied. The shapes of the signs were inspired by the curves of the wordmark's V and use the master Vancity gradient as a supporting graphic.

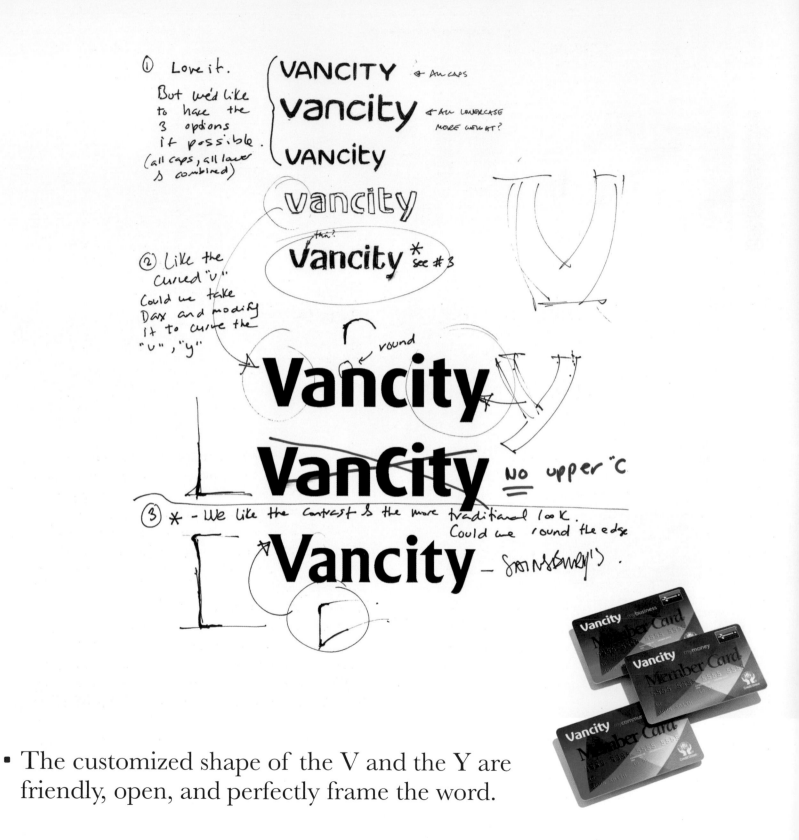

① Love it.
But we'd like to have the 3 options if possible. (all caps, all lower & combined)

VANCITY ← All caps

vancity ← All lowercase MORE WEIGHT?

VANCITY

vancity

Vancity * see #3

② Like the curved "v" Could we take Dax and modify it to curve the "v", "y"

round

Vancity

VanCity NO upper "C"

③ * — We like the contrast & the more traditional look. Could we round the edge — Sainsbury's.

Vancity

• The customized shape of the V and the Y are friendly, open, and perfectly frame the word.

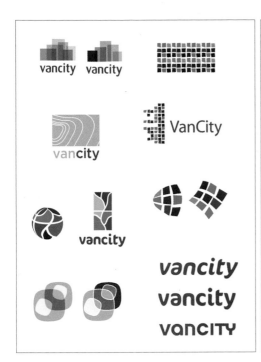

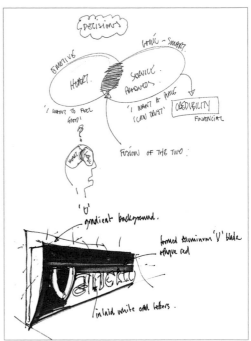

■ The designers explored many visual directions for the identity including ones that promoted Vancity as a multicultural community, as well as a company that is "at the heart of the community."

It also had the business expertise that allowed it to offer competitive advice, products, and services. The aim was to visually bring balance to this "heart + smart" equation that made Vancity so unique. One of the first steps taken was to remove the uppercase C in the original name, VanCity, which made it appear to be Vancouver-based. Vancity better reflected the extent of their presence throughout the province.

Although the brief called specifically for a wordmark, several routes were taken in developing a typographic logo. In the end, it was agreed that a wordmark would provide the best solution and would also allow for more creative room to build a creative platform in and around the mark.

LOGOS THAT DIDN'T CUT IT
Each of the logo-based alternatives presented to the client focused on a different aspect of the Vancity story, but they all shared the sense of humanity and optimism central to the brand. One suggestion included changing the brand's

corporate color from red to yellow—to move away from a category already crowded with red—and use a script inspired by an artist's signature. Although the client considered this, they believed the brand had equity in the color red. Other concepts played with the notion of Vancity as a reflection of a multicultural community by using mosaic imagery, while others showed Vancity as being at the heart of a community.

A FRIENDLY WORDMARK
The final result of the experimentation is a wordmark that truly reflects the brand's values and personality. The customized shape of the V and the Y are friendly, open, and perfectly frame the word. The brand color was changed to a brighter, more optimistic red that was more proprietary than the standard "retail red" (PMS 485). The resulting character of the mark positions Vancity as a welcoming financial institution that balances its emotive side with a confident business tone.

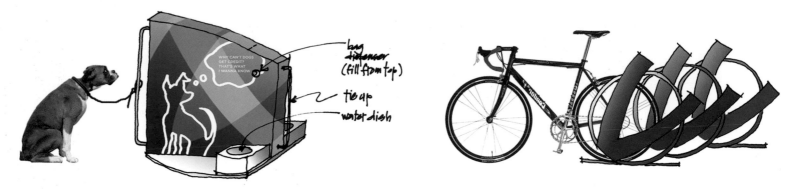

- The designers at Karacters felt strongly that the initial point of contact between the Vancity Credit Union and its customers should express the brand's unpretentious and welcoming personality.

THE CREATIVE PLATFORM

The concept of "being at the intersection" highlighted the fact that Vancity was present at pivotal moments in its member's lives—like buying a first home or retirement. A graphic using two intersecting V's expresses this idea visually. The intersections concept consequently took on additional meanings: as a representation of Vancity's interlacing financial services and, on a deeper level, an expression of Vancity's belief in bringing people together through their many community initiatives. Once the core gradient graphic was designed, it was used as a platform to differentiate the three aspects of the business: personal banking (red), business banking (blue), and community and environmental endeavors (green). This was further developed to include full-color palettes of secondary colors drawn from each gradient to provide a rich system for future applications.

GETTING CARDED

The client's new debit cards were a great example of how both the new personality and the gradient platform work.

To properly reflect the unique character of Vancity, a shift in tone was needed to create a more personal language. "My business," "my money," and "my community" were used to refer to each of the business segments in an empowering way.

TAKING IT TO THE STREETS

Vancity's research showed that its members weren't aware of the bank's extensive branch network. Plus, with no visual point of differentiation, the branches blended into the urban landscape. A signage system dramatically elevated Vancity's street presence and allowed the bank to take ownership of the highly visible locations it occupied. The shapes of the signs were inspired by the curves of the wordmark's V and use the master Vancity gradient as a supporting graphic. The overall campaign conveys a strong and consistent message, an essential quality for any financial institution.

The resulting character of the mark positions Vancity as a welcoming financial institution that balances its emotive side with a confident business tone.

■ The simple, solid, sans serif typestyle, the open spacing, and the house-shaped H give the inhaus logo a modern and clean look while conveying the company's housing-related flooring business.

STARTING FROM THE FLOOR UP

Formation Forest Products is a company owned by two Vancouverites with extensive backgrounds in the flooring industry. They wanted to launch a new venture for sourcing high-end flooring after discovering a laminate flooring product manufactured in Germany and soon began plans to import the floors to North America. They approached Grey Worldwide Northwest to help their company find its niche in the competitive shelter market. Grey was asked to develop a name and brand identity that would appeal not only to consumers but also to a group of prospective national dealers.

The designers suggested an identity that was modern, clean, and elegant but approachable to reinforce the brand character of high-end European design.

THE FOUNDATION FOR THE RIGHT NAME

The company needed a name that could differentiate it from its competitors while highlighting its focus on style and aesthetics. Because this category was primarily dominated by names reflecting a product or service's functional benefits, Grey ultimately decided that bucking this convention would provide the biggest impact. In addition, the new name would

DESIGN FIRM
GREY WORLDWIDE

CREATIVE DIRECTOR
JEFF LEWIS

DESIGNER
DAVID WONG

CLIENT
FORMATION FOREST PRODUCTS LTD.

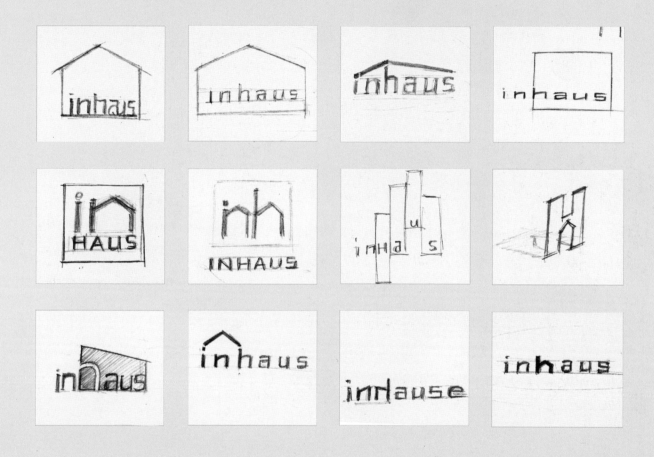

• Knowing that the brand's focus would always be on interiors, the team at Grey Worldwide Northwest recommended the name "inhaus" as a way to differentiate it from Martha Stewart and connote a high-end European design character.

What Are Laminate Floors?

Laminates are high performance floors made from wood. The top layer, known as the wear layer, protects against staining, fading and wearing. It is made from translucent paper (wood fibre), impregnated with moisture repelling resin and abrasion resistant aluminum oxide, which is roughly as hard as diamonds.

The next layer is a color image printed on specialty paper providing an authentic appearance. The core of the floor is a high density wood fibre panel that is extremely dent resistant. On the bottom of each plank is the balancing layer. This protects planks from bottom-up moisture and provides structural integrity. The result? A high performance floor with an unparalleled look and feel.

Installation

Our EasyConnect with Isowaxx system makes installation quick and clean. In fact, because it's glueless, you can walk and position furniture as soon as your floor is installed. In addition, Isowaxx seals the plank seams to make them even more moisture resistant.

Installation instructions are included in every box. If you would like more information, ask your retailer for a demonstration.

Cleaning and Care Instructions

inhaus floors are easy to keep clean - simply dust or vacuum, then wipe with a damp cloth and mild detergent. You probably have the necessary cleaning products already. For stubborn stain removal tips please refer to our Warranty and Care Information brochure.

Accessories

We offer a complete line of mouldings, trims and stair nosings as well as underlayment, cleaning and care products to complement your floor. Ask your retailer for information and samples.

• Choosing the inhaus name proved to be an extremely effective way of reinforcing that inhaus was the place to go for everything that could be found "in a house."

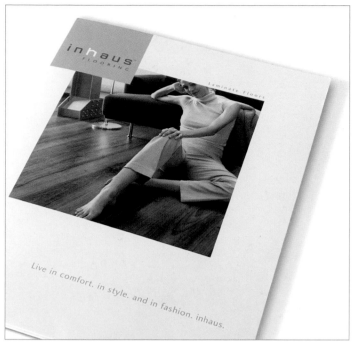

Working with a tight timeline and limited budget, Grey undertook a category investigation and uncovered some intriguing insights. One finding is that decisions on products such as flooring are usually driven by women, yet with the exception of only one product line, virtually all brands of flooring are positioned toward men.

require a certain level of flexibility to accommodate the company's plans to expand their product offerings beyond laminate flooring into related home interior products such as carpeting and paints.

Working with a tight timeline and limited budget, the designers immediately undertook a category investigation and uncovered some intriguing insights: decisions on products such as flooring are usually driven by women; with the exception of the Martha Stewart line, virtually all brands of flooring are positioned toward men.

Recognizing that the category is one traditionally viewed by women as a design accessory and that this brand's focus would always be on interiors, the team at Grey Worldwide Northwest recommended the name inhaus as a way to differentiate it from Martha Stewart and connote a high-end European design character. It was also an effective way of reinforcing that inhaus was the place to go for everything that could be found "in a house."

A SIMPLE WORDMARK APPROACH

The uncluttered house graphic forming the letter H is perfectly suited for this brand, which provides products that can make your home beautiful. The icon also works as an identity by itself. To complement the mark, the designers chose a simple, solid, sans serif typestyle with open spacing to give the logo a modern and clean look. Further supporting the style is a selection of subtle color schemes, that provide a warm and comfortable feeling.

The resulting graphic identity and design language has reinforced the positioning through its modern, austere, but decidedly warm look, making the inhaus brand immediately resonate with its urban target audience. From modest beginnings, the new brand name and identity design has been applied to print catalogs, point-of-sale displays, collateral, corporate communications, and the website with outstanding results. The combination of a flexible, unique, and simple approach was just the recipe for success the client had hoped for.

:: Capsoles

THE FIRST STEP

In 2004, after discussions with their patients and peers revealed the lack of orthotic footwear, two podiatrists set out to launch a new company that would fill that gap. In addition, research showed that although people spend a lot of time outdoors, the average person spends about 90 percent of their time indoors, 65 percent of which is spent at home. This information became the inspiration for developing the world's first EVA-injected, at-home podiatric clog. (Ethylene-vinyl acetate is a polymer that approaches elastomeric materials in softness and flexibility.)

Six months of research and development produced the first wooden mold of the product. The clients wanted to show a sample product made with this mold at one of its industry's largest trade shows. Although the final product would not be ready to display at the show, the goal was to launch the brand by introducing the innovative new product.

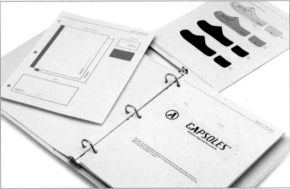

There are plenty of plastic gardening clogs in the marketplace, but the key differentiating factor for this one was that it was the only clog with true medical benefits. The Exhibit A design firm was not only excited about the product's potential, they knew it would be a great opportunity to show how design can add value to a product.

A QUICK TURNAROUND

To get ready for the trade show brand introduction, the creative team needed to complete the entire branding process in eight short weeks including naming, brand and identity development, color consultation, packaging, point-of-purchase material, promotional material (pens, apparel, brochures, prescription forms), trade show display materials, and an e-commerce website. As if that wasn't enough, the team was also working on the product design. After receiving the first batch of samples, Exhibit A produced a lengthy report

DESIGN FIRM
EXHIBIT A: DESIGN GROUP

CREATIVE DIRECTOR
CORY RIPLEY

DESIGNERS
CORY RIPLEY, ROBERT SPOFFORTH

CLIENT
DR. IAN YU

- As a new company, Capsoles wanted the visual identity to allow the name to resonate with its target audience. All typography and graphic elements needed to be simple.

• The Exhibit A design firm was not only excited about the product's potential, they thought it would be a great opportunity to show how design can add value to a product.

■ To create a consistent shelf presence, Exhibit A developed the wavy, dotted-line pattern as a key visual element for all of the Capsoles products. The corporate colors of cyan and cool gray were chosen to communicate the "sport-medical" concept.

■ The Capsoles brand signature consists of a stylized letter A (walking legs and arrow). When the symbol is used independently, it is contained in a circular form.

that outlined various alterations to the product and printed material preparation for final production. Product design alterations included an increase in the depth and width of the removable insole to achieve a smoother fit within the shoe, directions for the type of finish for the final product (matte versus shiny), and alterations for placement of the company's brand mark and symbol. The creative team also designed the ankle strap (including recommendations on the material to be used for it's production) and developed the idea for the "at-home" carrying bag, which was designed to add more value to the product.

The design team knew it would be a race to complete everything in time for the trade show, but when the workback, or critical path schedule was completed, they realized it was even tighter than they originally thought. They had less than a week to come up with a company name and the entire identity had to be completed within ten days to allow enough time for the materials to be produced overseas.

SEARCHING FOR THE RIGHT NAME

Five days into the project, Exhibit A presented the first short list of potential names to the client. Since there wasn't time to overanalyze the more than 400 names that were generated, the five that most relevant names were presented: Pediforms, Pods, Aegis, InSteps, and Capsoles.

In the end, the product's construction turned out to be the defining element in choosing the name. The clog is made up of two main parts: a protective toe box, or cap, and the foot bed, or sole of the shoe. Because of this, it was clear that Capsoles™ was the best fit for the brand. The next step was to visually convey the company's distinguishing brand characteristics, which were defined as functional, lightweight, modern, breathable, and movement.

A LEG UP ON LOGO DEVELOPMENT

For the first round of logo designs, Exhibit A focused on the feature characteristics of the product. Literal and nonliteral ideas were explored for a distinct and recognizable mark. The concepts included feathers and butterflies (lightweight and mobile); enclosed capsule shapes (protection), walking

■ From the original list of names proposed by the design team, the client chose the name Capsoles because the clogs are made up of two main parts: a protective toe box, or cap, and the foot bed, or sole, of the shoe.

legs and feet (movement and motion); and a variety of stylized letterforms. Both the designers and their client were immediately drawn to the idea of movement and motion.

Although they explored multiple typeface options for the wordmark, two typefaces they had used in concept designs were eventually chosen. The two typefaces used for the final design are a thinned-out version of Superduper Bold and Sophisto.

The Capsoles mark is composed of two elements: a symbol and a wordmark. Within the signature, a stylized letter A represents a nonliteral symbol for both walking legs and an arrow. The symbol can be featured within the wordmark or alone as a singular mark. When featured outside of the wordmark, the symbol is contained in a circular form to solidify and protect it. These options provide extreme flexibility when applied to various applications and are designed for optimal legibility at all sizes and in all situations. The wordmark is approachable and light, with the use of italic letterforms suggesting movement. It also appears simultaneously stable and energetic.

PUTTING IT IN STRIDE

Color also plays an important role in the creation of a brand. The Capsoles corporate colors (cyan and cool gray) were selected as the best combination to visually emote the term "sport-medical," with the added benefit of being easy to replicate in various methods of print production. An extended color palette allows for additional products to be included and provides the designer with options to tailor a completely new packaging experience for different consumer groups.

The wavy, dotted-line pattern is also a key visual element in achieving the overall brand impact while maintaining a consistent system. All products are noticeable on the shelves as a complete family and the modern graphic illustrates the brand's key characteristics of being lightweight, breathable, and promoting movement.

As a new company, Capsoles wanted the visual identity to allow the name to resonate with its target audience. All typography and graphic elements needed to be simple, so they opted not to include a tagline.

THE RESULT

The Capsoles brand adds value to the physical product, elevating it beyond a commodity. The company president realized the value of branding while attending the first trade show. Although the sample product had yet to arrive, the various printed and promotional materials were enough to make a strong impact with attendees from around the world.

- For the first round of logo designs, Exhibit A focused on the feature characteristics of the product. Literal and nonliteral ideas were explored for a distinct and recognizable mark.

GOING TOGETHER

When the Aboitiz Transport Group decided to integrate two of its smaller Philippines-based companies, Aboitiz One (a courier and transportation company) and WG&A (freight and logistics) were rebranded to create 2GO, an integrated logistics solutions provider. Offering a fully customizable suite of supply-chain solutions and services, 2GO's full-service brand positioning was defined as "a passion for delivery." Validated through a culture of dynamism and commitment to deliver, 2GO had the technology, network, and relationships to provide total supply-chain services across the Philippines.

With the brand positioning, FutureBrand developed key brand attributes as the building blocks of the 2GO brand by assigning behavioral characteristics. These attributes reflect the dynamic Filipino culture, focus on strong relationships with customers and trade partners, and accentuate the best-of-class distribution-channel management and technology that provide 2GO with the confidence and ability to deliver.

NAMING 2GO

The name 2GO was developed by FutureBrand to not only reflect the brand positioning, but also to capture the imagination of the local business population, where a perception gap existed between the capabilities of the local and international logistic companies.

The process of generating names started with applying a number of different filters during a series of work sessions. The names were then evaluated against the positioning and key imperatives for the brand. A final shortlist was presented to the board together with selection rationales. From the finalists, the senior management team unanimously selected 2GO as the preferred name.

■ FutureBrand's objective for naming this delivery company in the Philippines was to create a short, snappy noun that described the nature of the business. The immediacy of the brand is additionally reinforced in the logo's arrowhead.

DESIGN FIRM
FUTUREBRAND

CREATIVE DIRECTOR
CHARME SCOTT

DESIGNER
KIM KOKYU

CLIENT
ATS ABOITIZ TRANSPORT SYSTEMS

The 2GO visual communication system was designed to be visually arresting, simple to implement, and flexible enough to expand with the plethora of required applications.

2GO's 1,000 road vehicles, 200,000 containers, and fleet of planes act as a constant source of local pride, especially as a competitor to the more recognizable international players.

to accomplish great things we must not only act, but also dream; not only plan, but also believe...

a passion for delivery

2GO

■ The process magenta color was chosen for its simplicity, impact, and practicality and also took into consideration the many printing materials it would be applied to.

FutureBrand's objective behind the name was to create a short, snappy noun that could also be used as a verb when describing the service. "I need it 2GO" is the intended verbal articulation of the brand, which becomes an informed visual articulation. The arrowhead within the wordmark is another hook that reinforces the immediacy of the brand, but the visceral element within the identity system is the color; process magenta was selected for impact, simplicity and practicality—it can stand out in a sea of packaging. The color actually created a great deal of instant publicity. The production management was especially happy about the choice of process magenta because it would ensure consistency across its many disparate print applications, meeting the strict quality-control standards.

GOING WITH IT

The 2GO visual communication system was designed to be visually arresting, simple to implement, and flexible enough to expand with the plethora of applications required. 2GO first created a stir within the transportation networks of the Philippines as the dramatic magenta liveries freshened up the boring brown environment. The 1,000 road vehicles, 200,000 containers, and fleet of planes are a source of local pride, especially as a competitor to the more recognizable international players, who also tend to have name-driven identity systems.

Descriptive

Purely descriptive words cannot be trademarked but
they can very quickly communicate what the brand is
or does. The main problem with descriptive names is
that they can also promote your competitors. Although
these names tend to be very functional, they are also
too popular to be distinctive. Famous examples include
Bed Bath & Beyond and Holiday Inn.

:: Sydney Dance

GETTING A LEG UP

Frost Design was invited to create a new identity for the Sydney Dance Company. The brief was to create something distinctive and dynamic—an identity that had impact and recognition on a corporate level yet had enough flexibility to work with the promotional pieces used by the high-profile dance company at its numerous international performances.

A LOGO THAT MOVES

In redesigning the logo, Frost knew it needed to create an identity unique to both the Sydney Dance Company and to Sydney itself. Determined not to resort to something obvious or overtly dance related, the epiphany came when they realized that by adding two little letters to the word "Sydney" they could make it spell "dance." It was the ultimate creative gift: no other city in the world could promise such a solution.

DEVELOPING THE IDEA

Using Futura type as a base, the individual letters were made rounder and cleaner, creating a contemporary type solution that allowed the letters to "dance" while maintaining their legibility. A simple color differentiation also allowed the emphasis to be placed on the word "dance." Frost went on to develop a look and feel for the new identity, working with beautiful deep-toned images of dancers limbs interacting with the logo, creating a real sense of physical strength and movement across all their collateral materials. The Sydney Dance Company was delighted to begin 2006 with a new identity that positioned them as leaders on the international stage.

S Y D A N C E Y   C O M P A N Y

■ By simply adding two letters to the word Sydney, Frost Design achieved a simple creative solution to the Sydney Dance Company's logo by making Sydney "dance."

■ Beautiful deep-toned images of muscle-sculpted dancers' limbs were used in the dance company's brand identity to portray physical strength and movement.

DESIGN FIRM
FROST DESIGN

CREATIVE DIRECTOR
VINCE FROST

DESIGNERS
VINCE FROST, CAROLINE COX

CLIENT
SYDNEY DANCE COMPANY

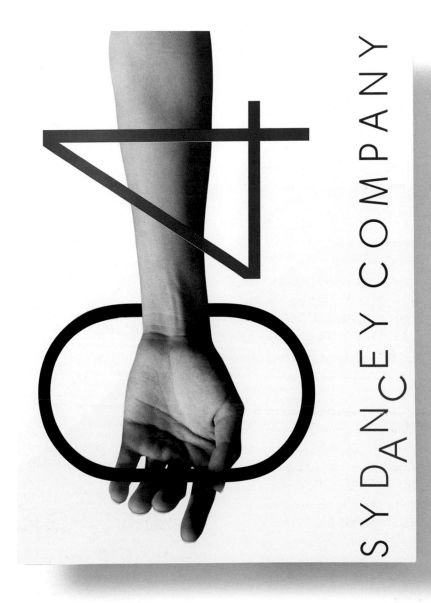

The brief was to create something distinctive and dynamic—an identity that had impact and recognition on a corporate level yet had enough flexibility to work with the promotional pieces used by the high-profile dance company at its numerous international performances.

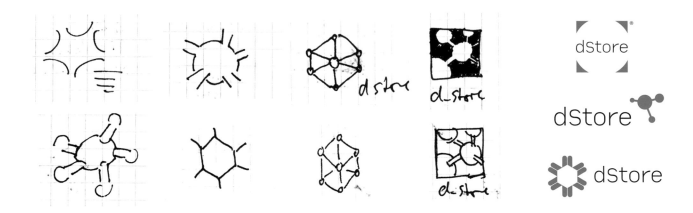

■ The H2D2 design firm was faced with the challenge of creating a logo for an e-business software product rather than a tangible one. They chose to represent the dStore software with stylized gearlike images that represent the modular nature of the e-commerce solution.

POSITIONING WITHOUT AN ACTUAL PRODUCT

dStore is an e-business solution for trading concerns and a supplier of branded articles. Their defining edge is the modularity of their software solution. dStore offers three variations of their software: one for bigger companies, one for small to medium-sized companies, and one that can grow with the client as its needs evolve. The goal of this project was to create a unique market position and distinguish the product from its competitors.

H2D2 began with extensive analysis of the structure and functionality of the product family. In cooperation with BOSIO1, an online marketing firm in San Francisco, they developed the name of the main product and its varying elements and functions. The name dStore was chosen because the "d" represents "dynamic," "difference," "digital," and "distribute," terms that are used in the general language used in product sheets, the website, etc, while the store portion of the name generates a direct connection to e-commerce. dStore is fundamental simplicity. dStore is up-to-date (compare to iTunes, etc).

DESIGN FIRM
H2D2

CREATIVE DIRECTOR
MARKUS REMSCHEID

DESIGNER
MARKUS REMSCHEID

CLIENT
DBAP GMBH

- Design agency H2D2 determined that the logo's design needed to have a modern look and feel in order to distinguish the product from its more traditional competitors.

• The firm developed a visual strategy based on an analysis of the corporate designs of dStore's competitors. H2D2's goal was to keep the corporate design simple and make the complex software understandable. The creative concept was to emphasize the product's ease of use by incorporating unnatural colors and childlike rounded shapes.

■ H2D2's designers incorporated the dStore logo into the company's collateral materials in a variety of ways, ranging from very straightforward placements to using it as a design element in arty ones, and some combined oversized and cropped versions such as on these presentation folders.

Following the name-development procedure, H2D2 analyzed the corporate designs of the competition and developed a visual strategy for the client. Design agency H2D2 determined that the logo's design needed to have a modern look and feel in order to distinguish the product from more traditional competitors in the marketplace. The design would also have to emphasize the product's ease of use. Based on this strategy, H2D2 chose a color palette that was fresh and modern. They specifically picked colors that would not appear in natural surroundings to emphasize the technical aspect of this product. The colors were also chosen to help increase the product's likeability and offer the impression that the software was easy and fun to use.

The real challenge was finding a symbol that could represent the dStore, a virtual product without a true visual reference. The final idea was to convey the idea of this software, which is used to build up an online shop, through a visual element. After a long development process, H2D2 found a graphic system that represented all of the aspects of the complex product family. The product has a modular structure so a modular image was incorporated into the final logo execution. The final logo not only represents the brand and the product but also provides a conceptual idea of the product's modular benefits.

PRESCRIBING A NAME

A free daily paper, more similar to a magazine than a newspaper, was to be launched in April 2005, catering to a younger readership (ages 18–34) with a focus on gossip and current events. The paper would offer both intellectual and pop culture content presented as short, digestible stories, with additional bits of facts and other trivia. The challenge was to create not only a name for the company but also a logo and layout built around the publication's personality.

Rethink's entire creative department, consisting of seven writers and thirteen designers, began the process by generating names. After developing a list of over 500 names aimed at conveying the paper's intellectual and pop culture content, the field was short-listed to four, which were presented to the client. The client immediately chose Dose, playing off the idea of a "daily dose."

THE PERFECT LOGO

The design team developed visual directions for the logo and brand identity. Concepts were sketched over a period of a few weeks, and after an intensive internal peer-review process, one direction was chosen as the clear solution and was the only one shown to the client. The logo was a natural: the capital D flipped horizontally creates a small capsule, representing the administration of information in small, bite-sized pieces.

The Wire

The Point

Dose

Dash

■ Rethink's creative team generated a list of over 500 possible names for the publication. Four of them—The Wire, The Point, Dose, and Dash—were short-listed and presented to the client, who immediately chose Dose—playing off the idea of a "daily dose."

■ The final logo cleverly flips a capital D horizontally to create a small capsule.

DESIGN FIRM
RETHINK

CREATIVE DIRECTORS
CHRIS STAPLES, IAN GRAIS

DESIGNER
JEFF HARRISON

CLIENT
DOSE

For the paper's layout, the designer set out to create a series of templates that visually broke up each page, making it look both accessible and readable. The goal was to make the paper feel modern, colorful, and vastly different from the traditional dailies.

The design team developed visual directions for the logo and brand identity. Concepts were sketched over a period of a few weeks and after an intensive internal peer-review process, one direction was chosen as the clear solution and was the only one shown to the client.

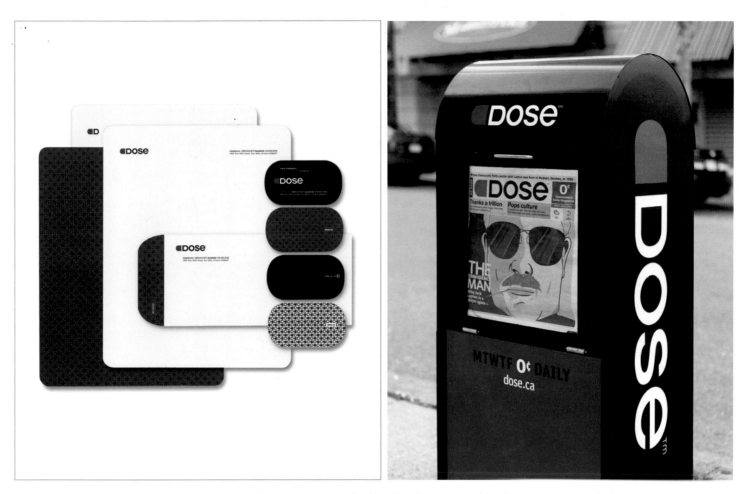

■ A free daily paper catering to a younger readership with a focus on gossip and current events needed a new name, visual identity, and all types of marketing vehicles from business cards to the display boxes in the street. Wherever possible, the designers echoed the logo's sideways D or capsule shape into the overall shape of marketing items such as the distribution boxes and letterhead system.

GETTING OFF THE GRID

For the paper's layout, the designer set out to create a series of templates that visually broke up each page, making it look both accessible and readable. The goal was to make the paper feel modern, colorful, and vastly different from the traditional dailies.

The capsule became an important element in the brand's identity, translated into the design of the distribution boxes, business cards, and promotional items. Despite two competitors arriving on the scene at the same time, Dose had an amazingly successful launch. The paper is well read with very high loyalty among its young demographic.

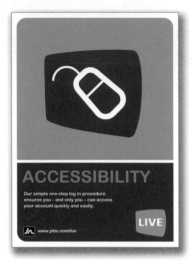

▪ JN Live's logo was designed to convey a vivid, diverse brand that is full of life, a mood that is enhanced by a varied and appealing color palette.

A HIP CONNECTION

The Jamaica National Building Society (JNBS) is one of Jamaica's largest financial institutions, but their conservative image made them eager to create a more youthful and modern image to increase their appeal to a younger audience. To do this, they took a unique approach and founded JN Live, a new service that gives customers four electronic channels (Internet, WAP, Telephone, and ATM) to conduct financial activities using a JNBS account in Jamaica and abroad. Though JNBS was not the first to offer these electronic channels, it was the first company in its market to bring these services to life for the consumer.

The design firm Karakter conducted research in Jamaica, which showed that leisure activities such as sports, music, dancing, and entertainment define much of the national identity, particularly for younger audiences. The brand strategy, therefore, did not focus on the new channels themselves, but rather on the lifestyles that they enabled and how the service put consumers in control of how they use their time. For example, although the service is said to provide a centralized point of interaction for banking needs, the feature it provides to its consumers is that it eliminates the need to physically visit a branch therefore not wasting time waiting in line.

DESIGN FIRM
KARAKTER

CREATIVE DIRECTOR
CLIVE ROHALD

DESIGNERS
KAM DEVSI, MARTIN WATKINS

CLIENT
JAMAICA NATIONAL BUILDING SOCIETY

- JNBS's conservative image made them eager to increase their appeal to a younger audience. They decided to use the JN Live sub-branding project as an opportunity to create a more youthful and modern image.

The brand strategy didn't focus on the new channels themselves, but rather on the lifestyles that they enabled and how the service put consumers in control of how they use their time.

■ The sans serif typeface reflects the informal attributes of the brand and allows for a
seamless application across billboards, websites, vehicles, and WAP-based applications.

The name JN Live was short listed together with JN Connect and JN 360. The word "Live"—underpinned by the tagline, "Get more out of life"—best expressed the customer benefits and the new corporate culture. It also played upon the two meanings and pronunciations of the word, both of which were both relevant for the brand.

A SYMBOL OF DIVERSITY

The final logo was designed as a family of logotypes in three color families, reflecting the simple and energetic attributes of the brand. JN Live was designed as a vivid, diverse brand that is full of life and with a varied and appealing color palette that further communicates that.

The JN Live typography was rendered as an informal sans serif typeface, expressing the lifestyle-simplifying attributes of the brand and encouraging a trial of JN Live's easy-to-use services. A key consideration in designing the logotype was the seamless application of the marks to different channels—from above-the-line billboard advertising campaigns to vehicle livery applications and from Web-based electronic media to the limitations imposed on applying the logotype to WAP-based applications such as cellular phones.

JN Live's new brand was launched at a trendy bar whose interior was decorated to fit with the brand's new image and distributing employee materials that explained the brand's character, tone of voice, and information on how to live the brand. The brand went live in August/September 2006, after this book went to press, so we can only assume it will be well received and provide JNBS with the hoped for results.

:: Solo Mobile

TALKING TO THE TARGET

Solo Mobile is all about youth. This division of Bell Canada was launched to bring tech-savvy friends together by using its cool phones and unique features such as 10-4 Nationwide Walkie-Talkie—a key for social function coordination. In essence, when you're with Solo, you're always with your friends.

With youth being the target audience (a hyperfickle consumer, even at the best of times) it was essential for Rethink to create a brand that was edgy, at times surreal, and visually striking. The message is simple: It's all about connectivity. With that in mind, the logo quite intuitively took the form of abstract digital connectors that weave in and out with exceptional visual dexterity. These distinctive connectors make the brand instantly recognizable and appropriate when translated across consumer touchpoints. From T-shirts to trucks and from TV advertising to packaging—the connectors are literally everywhere. In fact, the connectors are so well known, they're often seen without the Solo logo because they are able to offer instant brand recognition.

MAKING IT WORK TOGETHER

Rethink immersed itself in the culture of mobile technology—a jargon-filled, youth-influenced corner of the world—to create the solution. This was no small feat because their ultimate solution had to be extremely accessible and take into consideration where the identity would exist within the context of a larger telecom company. In other words, the idea had to be cerebral to the audience while being simple for the client.

The development of the creative came from a team of three designers dedicated solely to this project. With months of research behind them, the Rethink team spent approximately three weeks developing concept sketches for the logo. This entailed looking at every possible visual solution to the branding challenge at hand: make it surreal, make it cerebral,

■ The Solo Mobile division of Bell Canada was created to bring tech-savvy friends together by using its cool phones and unique features. The name Solo was chosen to convey the idea that when you're solo, you're still with your friends.

DESIGN FIRM
RETHINK

CREATIVE DIRECTORS
CHRIS STAPLES, IAN GRAIS

DESIGNER
JEFF HARRISON

CLIENT
SOLO

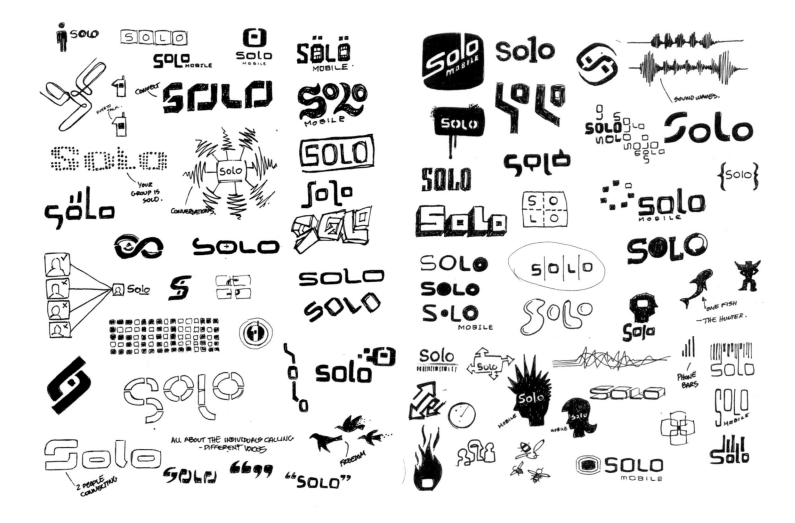

• With months of research behind them, the Rethink team spent approximately three weeks developing concept sketches for the logo. This entailed looking at every possible visual solution to the branding challenge at hand.

- The key was communicating the vision of the identity standards to all stakeholders and ensuring consistency in translating and applying the brand across all platforms.

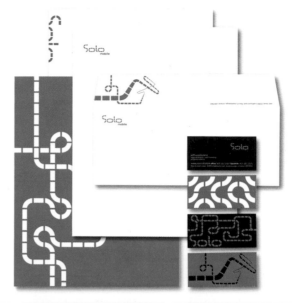

■ The Solo logo took the form of abstract digital connectors that weave in and out with exceptional visual dexterity. This concept lends an enormous amount of flexibility, as seen here in their dynamic letterhead system and website.

make it simple, and make it applicable across any and all potential media platforms.

After this exploratory work, the field was narrowed to the best possible strategic and visual solution. The idea (in rough format) was presented to the client, along with the rationale behind the thinking. The idea was approved on the spot.

The next several weeks were spent making refinements, illustrating typography, and developing the color palette. The letterforms were developed through a series of sketches in order to settle on details before the final was worked up in Illustrator, and optical tests were conducted at every stage to retain the detail of the connector points illustrations, even

when they were reproduced in small sizes. In total, over forty different illustrations were created for the system, each with its own message. The brand typeface, Galaxie Polaris, was chosen because of its simplicity and flexibility. Additionally, the character details in the typeface directly complement the Solo wordmark making it a seamless fit. For colors, the designers chose orange and black for their dramatic statement and because orange is reminiscent of the glow emitted from most walkie-talkies.

The end result of the designer's diligence is a campaign that is fresh, energetic, perfectly suited to its target audience, and memorable because of its meticulous consistency.

A TRADITIONAL LAUNCH

The creation of the Year of the Rooster logo was requested by the Lubbock Chinese American Association (LCAA) for their four holiday festivals in 2005, the Year of the Rooster. A nonprofit organization, LCAA's mission is to promote Chinese culture in mainstream American society.

The logo was intended to increase interest and participation in traditional Chinese festivals; therefore, the client requested a fun, playful message to stimulate excitement about the events. The use of color in this piece conveys the convivial festival atmosphere.

BUILDING ON A THEME

The theme of the logo was "East Meets West." The two components of the logo—the year 2005 and the image of a rooster—were combined with an Asian-inspired type treatment, achieved by creating the words with brushstrokes used to draw Chinese characters. Since the final audience included both Chinese and Americans, legibility was a major concern during the ideation process. To make the words easy to read without sacrificing the look of the compelling visual, different colors were incorporated.

With the nonprofit's small budget, full-color printing would have been too expensive, limiting them to printing with just two colors. To overcome this challenge, the designers used the logo in different color combinations used on varying background colors of different materials. For instance, the client decided to print all the invitations on red paper (a tradition in Chinese culture) in order to create an inviting festival atmosphere, with the logo printed in gold but the event programs were printed on white paper with a red logo.

The overall look of the final logo is fresh and contemporary while paying homage to its Chinese roots and representing the organization in a tasteful manner.

■ As with many nonprofits, a slim budget limited the organization to two-color printing. In order to overcome this challenge, the designers livened up the materials by incorporating various colored and white paper stocks with the logo running in different colors.

■ To increase interest in the holiday events taking place while celebrating the Chinese Year of the Rooster, the Lubbock Chinese American Association (LCAA) commissioned this logo for all the event materials.

DESIGN FIRM
CHEN DESIGN

CREATIVE DIRECTOR
CHEN WANG

DESIGNERS
CHEN WANG, DIRK FOWLER

CLIENT
LUBBOCK CHINESE AMERICAN ASSOCIATION

An Asian-inspired type treatment was achieved by creating the words with strokes used to draw Chinese characters.

:: Modular

CONNECTING WITH AN AUDIENCE

Soulsight believes that when developing a brand it is imperative to highlight the values that help it connect with its audience. Their detailed research and analysis of relevant markets provides insight to determining the story they need to tell to capture their target audience's attention.

For this project, Soulsight's primary objective was a daunting one: to create a name and an identity that would help a social initiative be considered by the top government authorities of developing nations. To achieve this, the brand had to reflect the socially responsible nature of the project and the actual product being offered—modular housing units. This meant that many factors, including the company's business plan and even their choice of interlocutors, would play a major role in defining the appropriate look and feel for the brand.

A NAME THAT BUILDS INTEREST

Beginning with the name, Soulsight deemed it essential for the name to reflect the intrinsic benefits of the product for both functional and legal purposes. The brilliance of the product revolved almost entirely around its modular characteristics, so they selected the name Modular—a simple yet effective name that addressed the client's criteria. The name could also be easily extended, allowing for the development of a naming convention that could be applied to the different housing units being offered: Modular 30m, Modular 50m, and Modular 60m.

PUTTING IT ALL TOGETHER

Modular's visual identity needed to illustrate the socially responsible nature of the product, including its pledges to sustainability and environmental awareness. Encompassing the need to convey a serious message, the brand was positioned as elegant, discreet, and sober, while remaining mindful of its modern aesthetic, allowing the brand's genuine personality to appeal to world leaders.

■ Soulsight's designers created an identity that conveyed the modern and minimalist sensibility of this modular housing unit company. Modular's stylishly cool, clean logo appears on all its collateral materials, resulting in a handsome, contemporary and very sophisticated look.

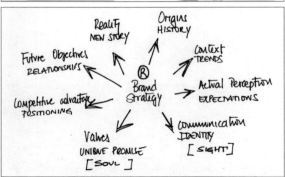

■ In order to create a compelling visual identity, the designers analyzed all facets of the company to determine which direction would result in the strongest brand strategy.

DESIGN FIRM
SOULSIGHT

CREATIVE DIRECTOR
LUIS HERNÁNDEZ

DESIGNER
LUIS HERNÁNDEZ

CLIENT
MODULAR

- Modular's visual identity needed to illustrate the socially responsible nature of the product including its pledges to sustainability and environmental awareness. The brand was positioned as elegant, discreet, and sober, while remaining mindful of its modern aesthetic.

THE NAMING PROCESS

Encode is a leading systems integration firm and premiere IBM business partner. In 1997, when short, one-word company names seemed to dominate the landscape, the company's founder, Jerry Sforza, generated the name for his company. "What single word describes what we do?" He thought "Code" was the obvious choice, but seemed short and impersonal. After some thinking, Sforza's wife suggested Encode. It suggested the action of the programming process with a softer, more pleasant-sounding name. Sforza was attracted to the simplicity, honesty, and directness of the approach.

A TRADITIONAL APPROACH

Over time, Encode outgrew its original identity and felt it no longer properly reflected the company's status in the industry. So the design agency Flat set out to update the mark. While Encode operates in the high-tech field, Flat didn't want the mark to have a tech-heavy feel. They employed a visual technique that provided a sense of tradition. By designing a classic mark, such as IBM of the 1950s, rather than referencing today's branding of the tech industry, the logo makes the company look as if it has existed for decades.

The interlocking letters of the logo stem from Encode's core practices of encryption, security, and system mergers. The attached or overlapping letter shapes symbolize their expertise—two objects that are interlocked, connected, and merged. The designers explain: "Self-contained objects that come together to form a system are things you find everywhere in nature. We're enforcing that connection by using microscopic imagery of materials and molecular structures throughout their communications material." The modular CO can be separated from the mark and used as a freestanding symbol for signage and merchandise, making this flexible system a powerful tool for branding communication.

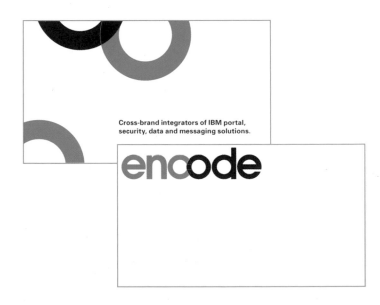

■ The interlocking letters of the logo stem from Encode's core practices of encryption, security, and system mergers. The attached or overlapping letter shapes symbolize their expertise—two objects that are interlocked, connected, and merged.

DESIGN FIRM
FLAT

PROJECT MANAGER
DOUG LLOYD

DESIGNERS
PETTER RINGBOM, HOLLY GRESSLEY

CLIENT
ENCODE

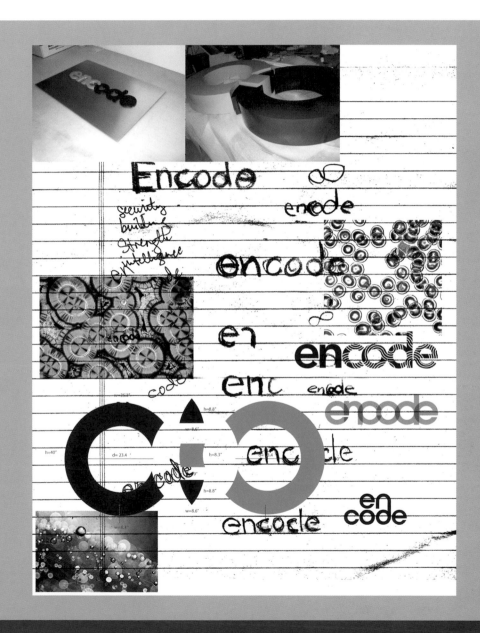

The modular CO in the center of the logo can be separated from the mark and used as a freestanding symbol for signage and merchandise.

■ Mortensen created a visual that reflects the nature of Dept B's service—the back office or the other side of the business. The bright and upbeat versions of the chosen colors were an obvious fit. Blue stands for trustworthiness, knowledge, calm, and peace; while green represents money, healing, growth, and success.

THE BIG PICTURE

PM&R was a small bookkeeping firm with a big idea. It wanted to become the nation's leading provider of back-office services for small medical practices. There was only one problem—the name PM&R (besides being opaque and unmemorable), is an abbreviation for Physical Medicine and Rehabilitation, a medical specialty that was no longer the company's focus.

It turns out that most small-office doctors lose a surprising amount of their income to uncollected bills, badly handled insurance claims, and poor bookkeeping skills. By outsourcing their bookkeeping to a company like PM&R, they can increase their revenues by 20 percent or more. What PM&R was looking for was a way to package concepts such as bookkeeping, outsourcing, close partnering, and friendliness into a new identity.

THE BIG IDEA

The identity firm Mortensen Design enlisted the brand consulting services of Neutron and the two firms began a collaborative effort to develop a name and trademark, along with other communications vehicles, which would reposition PM&R. They started by working back and forth on names. ("Out-practice would be hard to pictorialize—but Profitree works." "Okay then, how about B-keepers—you've got bees, hives, men in white suits.") Eventually, the identity firm, and the branding firm, together with the client, got the selection down to a dozen names that had both graphic potential and URL domain name availability.

The name Department B was chosen because of its storytelling potential. (What does the B stand for? Business, back office, bookkeeping, billing.) The elevator pitch—a brief overview of an idea for a product, service, or project that

DESIGN FIRM
MORTENSEN DESIGN, INC.

CREATIVE DIRECTOR
GORDON MORTENSEN

DESIGNERS
GORDON MORTENSEN, CHRIS ROSSI, PATRICIA MARGARET

CLIENT
DEPARTMENT B

- The elevator pitch (a brief overview of an idea for a product, service, or project that can be delivered in the time span of an elevator ride) for Dept B is that it frees up physicians' hands so they can practice medicine instead of business.

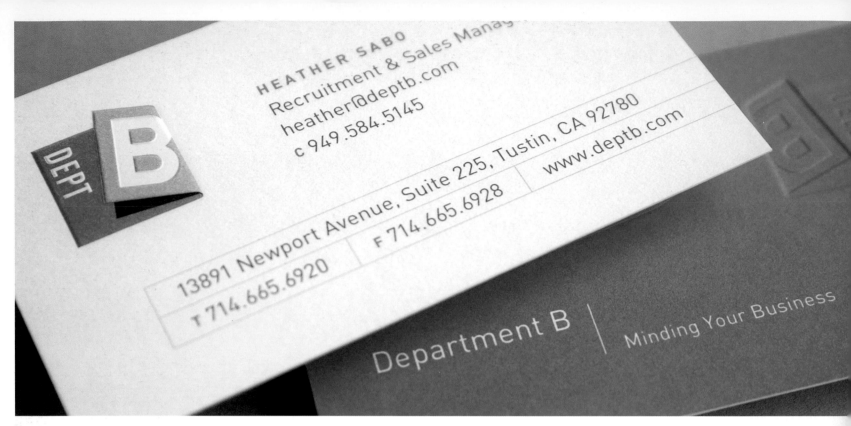

■ The name Department B was chosen for this medical bookkeeping company because of its storytelling potential. What does the B stand for? Business, back office, bookkeeping, billing, etc.

can be delivered in the time span of an elevator ride—for Department B is that it frees physicians' hands so they can practice medicine instead of business "Stop worrying about business," it goes. "That's our department." And what is the advertising tagline? "Department B. Minding your business."

CRAFTING THE VISUAL

The Mortensen Design team began by creating a series of wordmark and monogram ideas. Several of the monogram ideas were encouraging, especially those that incorporated an additional visual device such as a door, a plus sign, an arrow, etc. However, when the ideas were spread out for review, they realized something was missing. None of the ideas said Department B is the back office (the other side of the business). Going back to the drawing board, they devised a square with one edge folded back revealing a contrasting trapezoid shape with a white letter B. The client liked the idea right away and didn't want to consider any alternatives;

they had made their decision. "Move forward. How soon can we see it in color?"

As it turned out, applying the color was the most challenging part of the process. The client couldn't settle on any of the seventy-five color combinations presented and those that had potential were either too close to colors being used by their competitors or they didn't agree with the designer's sense of aesthetics. Plan B was to explore the meanings of colors and this is when the answer became clear. Blue stands for trustworthiness, knowledge, calm, and peace; while green represents money, healing, growth, and success. In addition, the green colors were bright and upbeat.

The final mark works because it is memorable and immediately conveys the value of Department B's service—a successful medical practice is a close partnership between the front office and the back office.

· PM&R (now Dept B) was a small bookkeeping firm with a big idea. It wanted to become the nation's leading provider of back office services for small medical practices.

Invented

Names that are completely made up are the easiest to trademark
but are also the most difficult to remember. Invented names
require people to form new associations—this is both an
opportunity and a challenge. Invented names tend to demand
greater marketing budgets but also have the greatest potential to
define a new category. That's exactly what Xerox did.
Famous examples include Kodak and Pepsi.

TERRAVIDA COFFEE®

■ Although concerned about how it would reproduce across many surfaces, to stand out in their category, the TerraVida café chose a textured wordmark that transforms the letters A and V into a plantlike shape that refers to its eco-consciousness. The mottled surface adds a warm and friendly antiqued finish that is also a natural complement to the café's overall natural theme.

■ The juxtaposition of nature and lifestyle photographs is incorporated into the packaging graphics, depicting the interconnection between the land and life.

CAFFEINATED CONCEPTS

The Hornall Anderson design team began the TerraVida Coffee project by agreeing with the client on a brand positioning statement. While the positioning informed the naming, graphics, and store architecture, it also served as a good reference at every design presentation to make sure the designs adhered to the client's values and goals. The positioning focused on three brand promises: they were a high-end specialty retailer, their coffee was grown and produced using environmentally responsible means, and the café would be a place where their customers could communicate and connect, whether with each other, the barista, or the day's news.

THE NAME AND LOGO

Hornall Anderson hired Pamela Mason-Davey, a talented namer and writer, to explore names for the cafe. She presented them with thirty to forty names broken down into five categories: Conscience, Energy, Origins, Character, Myth, and Personal. In choosing a name, it was important to reflect the client's value as a high-end specialty retailer whose product, coffee, was grown and produced using environmentally responsible means. It was also important to convey that the cafe would be a place where customers could communicate and connect.

The chosen name TerraVida came from the category referred to as Origins. This category reflected names that put coffee in the context of where it is grown and helped connect one audience (American coffee drinkers) with another (small farmers from around the world). TerraVida was chosen because it is a direct translation in Latin of "earth" and "life."

DESIGN FIRM
HORNALL ANDERSON DESIGN WORKS

CREATIVE DIRECTOR
JACK ANDERSON

DESIGNERS
SONJA MAX, JAMES TEE, TIFFANY PLACE,ELMER DELA CRUZ, JANA NISHI

CLIENT
TERRAVIDA COFFEE

• Hornall Anderson collaborated with architectural firm GGLO on the design of the TerraVida retail store. From the beginning, GGLO approached the store design very conceptually, expressing the combination of land and life through various materials and structural elements.

• A bold color palette and dynamic imagery are used across all of TerraVida's packaging, lending a unique energy to the store and its products.

■ The final design for the TerraVida store is a holistic illustration of how the land supports life. The earth-tone architectural land elements of the store are contrasted with the brightly colored elements of the menu board.

The first design presentation consisted of nine different logo interpretations of the TerraVida name. Guided by Mason-Davey's categories, some focused on graphic simplicity and symbolism, others were more organic with rough-hewn texture, and others incorporated animal imagery. These logos were all accompanied by details such as a coffee cup, color palette, photography, or illustration styles that would give more meaning to the logo and help the client understand the look and feel that would go with a particular wordmark.

A WARM AND FRIENDLY FEELING

Although the client was concerned about the reproducibility of a textured wordmark, they wanted it to stand out visually in the cluttered café category. Their desire to be unique allowed them to choose a memorable logo far more valuable than a flat, two-dimensional wordmark. The texturing adds a patina that is warm and friendly. The juxtaposition of nature and lifestyle photographs is incorporated into the packaging graphics, depicting the interconnection between the land and life.

Hornall Anderson collaborated with architectural firm GGLO on the TerraVida retail store. GGLO approached the store design very conceptually, expressing the combination of land and life through various materials and elements. Some drawings had the café literally split in two—the bottom half representing Earth and the top half representing life.

The final store design is a holistic illustration of how the land supports life. The earth-tone architectural land elements of the store are contrasted with the brightly colored elements of the menu board, a vivid hand-off area, and inventive fossil beds—the life elements. The fossils are a humorous twist on modern life, with impressions of a pacifier, wristwatch, cell phone, and sunglasses that are labeled Carpool, Day Care, Budget Meeting, Dry Cleaner, Soccer Practice, Dentist Appointment, PTA Meeting, and finally, TerraVida Caramel Latte. The fossils arose out of a desire to draw the customers into the experience of the space, granting them an extra moment or two to explore. This exploration gives customers time to contemplate the role (or absence) of nature in their own lives so they understand that TerraVida cares about its customers and the planet.

A SPIRITED HISTORY

SEA's involvement in the branding of a new restaurant and cocktail lounge began in an unusual way. Their client, the restaurant owner Mark Chan; the restaurant's architect, Jeremy Walker from Hawkins Brown; and John Simpson from SEA were instructed to meet at the movie theater The Screen on the Green in Islington, London, to watch the animated film *Spirited Away*. This was to be part of the inspiration for OQO, Chan's latest venture.

A WELL-ROUNDED CONCEPT

Chan wanted a name that had no meaning and that was simple, short, and symmetrical. He was also determined to have a visually driven identity that could be used as a template for the other bars and restaurants he intended to open in the future.

The bar and restaurant primarily serves signature cocktails and unique Chinese tapas, so the creative team selected images of specific foods and drinks that echoed the circular forms of the logo. The photographs detailed the forms, colors, and textures of the unusual flavors and ingredients found on OQO's menu. Using photographic images throughout the interiors of the bar and on individual user-friendly items such as menus, matchboxes, posters, and coasters gave a sexy yet food-focused identity to OQO's environment. The success of this identity also owes much to the designers' ability to incorporate a number of disciplines including architecture, graphic design, and photography.

■ The client was especially interested in having a visually driven identity that could be applied when they expanded to other bars and restaurants, so the assignment was to create a name that was simple, short, symmetrical, and had no real meaning at all.

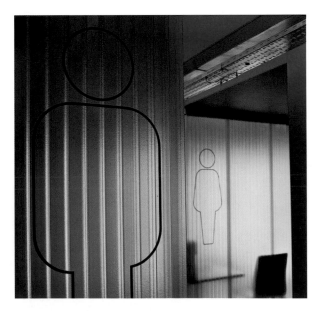

■ The rounded icons for OQO's restrooms echo the circular theme carried out in the restaurant's logo and graphics.

DESIGN FIRM
SEA

CREATIVE DIRECTORS
JOHN SIMPSON, BRYAN EDMONDSON

DESIGNER
JAMIE ROBERTS

CLIENT
OQO

• The success of this identity owes much to the designers' ability to incorporate a number of disciplines including architecture, graphic design, and photography.

Using photographic images throughout the interiors of the bar and or individual user-friendly items like menus, matchboxes, posters, and coasters gave a sexy yet food-focused identity to OQO's environment. The photographs detailed the individual forms, colors, and textures o the foods and ingredients found on OQO's menu.

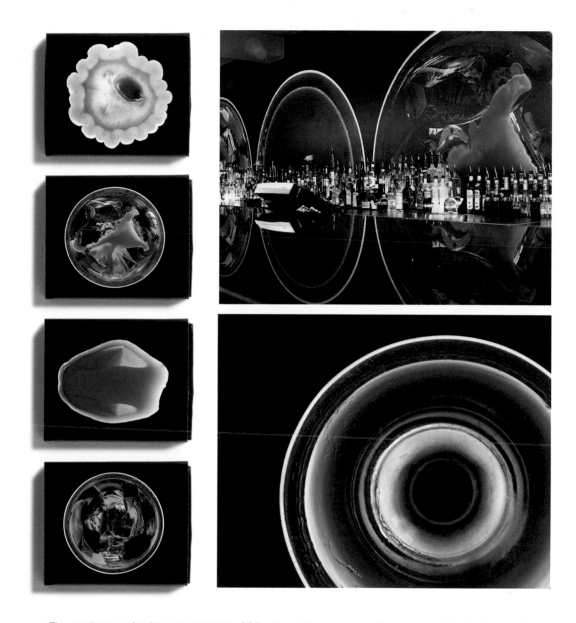

■ The creative team for this new restaurant, OQO, selected images of specific food and drinks that echoed the circular forms of the logo. These dynamic photographs were carried throughout the brand's touch points such as on matchbooks and on the oversized graphics placed behind the bar.

:: Circ

A NEW GLOBAL BRAND FOR MEN

In 1998, Procter & Gamble developed a breakthrough product that gave the appearance of a fuller, thicker head of hair—a proposition considered to be especially appealing to men affected by hair loss.

While Dew Gibbons wanted the brand name and design to have a contemporary resonance, they also wanted it to have a degree of anonymity, to not shout about itself or the product's principal benefit. They also didn't want the brand to be apologetic in any way. So a modern, contemporary, minimalist design positioned the brand as a positive beauty care choice, while still relatively understated.

Initial creative work defined "retaking control" of one's personal appearance as the brand positioning. Briefed on the consumer's perspective, the design team gained useful insights into the male psyche and quickly understood the key motivations of the target audience. They knew the name should express the desire of men who were losing their hair to retake control of their appearance—coming full circle, returning to looking and feeling confident. The Circ name survived the rigorous legal process necessary for a global launch and then the graphic identity developed naturally as a holistic expression of the circular imagery, which also evokes locks or curls of hair.

GROWING A NEW BRAND IDENTITY

Dew Gibbons undertook the name and identity creation, working closely with Procter & Gamble throughout all stages of the project to establish the Circ personality across brand-building media. This included the brand's website (created principally to drive trial use of the product) along with a broader range of materials used to launch the brand in other channels.

B10G	aka	cobalt	manus
181 C	m & b	gene b	man-ic
42	m & co	true	reef
m²	circ.	blue note	tank
cuso₄	men & co	blue shift	man-made
²fold	blä	deep	m.code

As illustrated here, the designers explored many directions before selecting the final look for this new hair-treatment product. The Circ name expresses the process of "retaking control" and completing the circle. While the designers at Dew Gibbons wanted the brand design to have a contemporary resonance, they also wanted it to have a degree of anonymity. The minimal approach positions the brand as a positive beauty care choice while still appearing relatively understated.

DESIGN FIRM
DEW GIBBONS

CREATIVE DIRECTORS
SHAUN DEW, STEVE GIBBONS

DESIGNERS
SUZANNE LANGLEY, JACQUI OWERS

CLIENT
PROCTER AND GAMBLE

• Circ's minimalist logo was designed to convey the idea of coming full circle, returning to looking and feeling confident, to their key market: men experiencing hair loss.

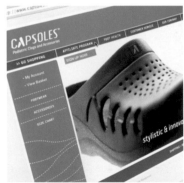

Metaphorical

Names that are evocative or that borrow from stories, cultural icons, or other emotive forces are classified as metaphorical. These names have the power to create instant associations with desired themes, feelings, and ideas. They also tend to be able to extend into a variety of categories without diluting their essence. Famous examples include Virgin and Apple.

A NAME WITH A VIEW

What do you call a restaurant that sits high above the water, has a killer view of Vancouver's Stanley Park, and is sure to serve up a good time? These restaurateurs had struggled with a name for some time before coming to the WOW agency for help. The restaurant's owners knew they had secured a stunning location, but they needed a name that was equally inspiring.

One of the restaurant's owners told WOW a story that struck a chord: he was standing on the platform where the restaurant was to be built and imagined he was on a cruise ship slowly making its way out to sea as the sun set. Then he asked WOW to imagine the excitement of the people on board the ship as the waving, envious onlookers watched them. "I want people to feel like they're on that ship," he said. "Our location and architecture will do it, but I really want to capture it in the name."

WOW's designers printed out that story and posted it around the office. To begin the creative process of generating naming ideas, they surrounded themselves with imagery of the location, architectural renderings, and pictures of cruise ships.

The name Lift actually came to one of the WOW creatives on his way to the gym—proof that good ideas are everywhere. Back at the office, he asked if anyone had been to the new restaurant around the corner called Lift. People responded well to the name, saying it would definitely have been appropriate for the project—too bad, it was taken. It was a sneaky ploy, but it worked.

■ After an extensive study of typefaces, a clean serif type was chosen for its timelessness. Working closely with architectural and interior design renderings, the design team combined bold colors with the elegance of the typeface.

DESIGN FIRM
WOW BRANDING

CREATIVE DIRECTOR
PERRY CHUA

DESIGNERS
WILL JOHNSON, JEFF SCHRAMM

CLIENT
LIFT

Using the "Bar Grill View" descriptor, WOW set a classic and sophisticated tone for the restaurant.

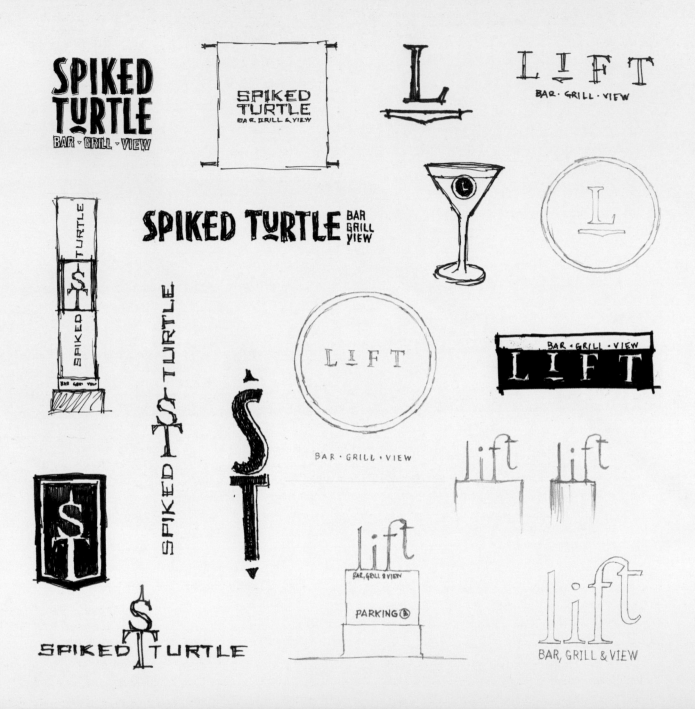

A concept that ultimately was not chosen incorporated a whimsical type treatment with the T literally lifted into the air.

■ The floating letters in the Lift logo play on the restaurant's promise of a positive and uplifting dining experience, while the color story draws inspiration from the rich fabrics and natural materials used throughout the building.

WOW's designers knew they wouldn't be able to present the new name to the client on a white piece of paper; they had to sell it. In order for it to be accepted, the restaurant's owners needed to see their restaurant, not just a word. The creative team decided to fully develop the identity, including signage, chef uniforms, business cards, and even embossed cutlery, to make it real for the owners. They then created a keynote presentation (with music to set the mood) to make the conceptual restaurant come alive.

GIVING LIFT A BOOST

The conceptual restaurant was described as a high-end bar and grill with a breathtaking panoramic view. Using the "Bar Grill View" descriptor, WOW set a tone that was classic and sophisticated. After an extensive study of typefaces, a clean serif type was chosen for its timelessness. Working closely with architectural and interior design renderings, the design team combined bold colors with the elegance of the typeface, creating a brand identity that complemented the interior space and the building's striking exterior.

■ When the WOW agency presented the owners of the restaurant with a concept, it included more than just designs for the name and logo. The designers decided to fully develop the identity, including signage, chef uniforms, business cards, and even embossed cutlery, to make it real for the owners.

The floating letters in the logo play on the restaurant's promise of a positive and uplifting dining experience, while the color story—deep black and metallic silver with a rust orange—draws inspiration from the rich fabrics and natural materials used throughout the building. A concept that was ultimately not chosen incorporated a whimsical type treatment with the T literally lifted into the air. While inviting and playful, the concept lacked the sophistication that the five-star waterfront establishment demanded.

DOUBLE CONCEPTS

Two names and identities (Lift and Spiked Turtle) were presented to the client along with a signature martini for each.

Two names were presented because the staff was violently split over which one would be best.

The name Spiked Turtle was discovered when team members were asked to think up words that conjured up strong imagery. The words "spiked" (alcoholic, sharp, edgy) and "turtle" (laid-back, hard shell, retreat) conveyed a funky bar-type atmosphere and had a lot of potential for creative expression.

The client loved Lift. It was the ideal name for a brand identity that evoked both the soaring architecture and the aspirations of the restaurateurs. The food, the people, and the location are all designed to give you a "lift."

The restaurant's owners knew they had secured a stunning location—but they needed a name that was just as inspiring.

▪▪ Eastern Hotel

▪ The bathroom ceilings on the Pacifica level of the Eastern Hotel in Sydney are covered in images taken by Australian photographer Warwick Orme, which have a simplicity and sensuality perfect for the intimate environments.

RESTORING AN IDENTITY

Inspired by the great Art Deco hotels of the 1930s, the Eastern Hotel in Sydney was reborn as a grand hotel with interiors by renowned SJB Interiors. The Layfield agency was commissioned to create a new strategy and brand identity for both the hotel and the individual identities of each floor, including signage, menus, stationery, and graphics.

The challenge Layfield faced was uniting four different experiences under one umbrella brand, while allowing each floor to communicate its own personality. Using Art Deco motifs as a starting point, Layfield created four different themes, uniting them with three common elements—typeface, color, and pattern.

Each floor of the hotel has its own distinct combination of two colors. For example, the Eastern Bar picks up the peacock blue of the original tile columns and contrasts it with the deep bronze of the decorative panels, while the Ruby Lounge plays upon the Chinese red and black of its furniture and fittings. Original Art Deco patterns were sourced to reflect the personality of each floor, from the Pacific palm tree design of the Classic Bar & Diner to the intricate Chinese diamond lattice pattern of the Ruby Lounge. The patterns are used as subtle varnishes on menu covers and etched onto windows and glass surfaces.

To unite the levels, Layfield used architect Richard Neutra's classic 1930s typeface, Neutraface; its linear geometry coupled with an unmistakably warm and human feel was chosen for its elegance, simplicity, and its ability to work across all four identities. It was important for the typeface to have an Art Deco feel, but it needed to avoid the decorative nature of many of the display alphabets. A simple typeface was required to complement the intricate patterns, yet at the same time, it had to have enough character to work by itself as a beautiful piece of type on numerous applications such as the stationery.

Similarly, silver and gloss black are common to all levels, on external and internal signage and on coasters and

DESIGN FIRM
LAYFIELD

CREATIVE DIRECTOR
STEPHEN LAYFIELD

DESIGNER
STEPHEN LAYFIELD

CLIENT
THE EASTERN HOTELS GROUP

• Silver and gloss black are common to all levels, on external and internal signage and on coasters and matchboxes.

The Bordello is a red-curtained room with an expansive red leather bed and a mirrored ceiling. The room really couldn't have been called anything else!

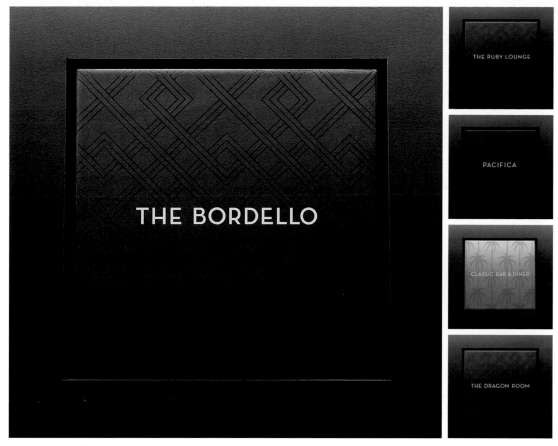

THE BORDELLO

THE RUBY LOUNGE

PACIFICA

CLASSIC BAR & DINER

THE DRAGON ROOM

▪ To unite the different levels of the hotel, Layfield used the same type—architect Richard Neutra's classic 1930s typeface, Neutraface—chosen for its elegance, simplicity, and its ability to work across the separate identities on each of the hotel's four floors.

matchboxes, but each floor has its own distinct combination of two additional colors that are reflective of their theme. The Eastern Bar, for example, picks up the Peacock blue of the original tiled columns in contrast with the deep bronze of the decorative panels. The colors are used on the menus and the ceramic signage tiles, providing solid blocks of color that unite all areas of the interior.

COMMUNICATING IDENTITY THOUGH INTERIOR DETAILS

Layfield commissioned the Art Deco–inspired tiles from ceramicist Warren Moorfoot of Clay Graphics, who was already replacing damaged tiles in the building. Moorfoot sourced the tiles in the correct colors and screen printed them with a pattern and white type before glazing and firing.

The bathrooms added distinctive character to further differentiate each level's theme. For example, the bathrooms in the Classic Bar & Diner continue the 1930s Pacific Rim look with a twist. Each of the five cubicles in the women's bathroom holds a vintage travel poster by artist Kerne Erickson. The hand-drawn typography on the posters is replicated on circular silver discs on the doors, echoing the shape of the mirrors and effectively naming each cubicle.

On the Pacifica level, the bathroom ceilings are covered in images taken by Australian photographer Warwick Orme. (Layfield had recently designed Orme's book, *Floranova*, for Random House and persuaded the photographer to provide his unique images for the project.) Orme's images have a simplicity and sensuality perfect for the intimate

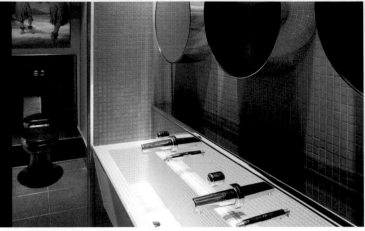

■ The bathrooms in the Classic Bar & Diner continue the 1930s Pacific Rim look with a twist. Each of the five cubicles in the women's bathroom holds a vintage travel poster by artist Kerne Erickson. The hand-drawn typography on the posters is replicated on circular silver discs on the doors, echoing the shape of the mirrors and effectively naming each cubicle.

environments: a pink phalanopsis orchid cascades across the women's bathroom ceiling and the men's bathroom is littered with luminous oak leaves.

THE NAME GAME

THE EASTERN
In the context of the 1930s, the Eastern Hotel evokes the Far East—glamorous, mysterious, and exotic. The hotel is also situated in the heart of Sydney's affluent Eastern Suburbs.

THE EASTERN BAR
The ground-floor bar derives its name from the hotel and is logically called the Eastern Bar.

CLASSIC BAR & DINER
During the initial concept stage, the second floor's central Art Deco bar and diner-style banquettes were affectionately referred to as "the Diner." It was decided that "Diner" should be incorporated into the final name. The name Classic Bar & Diner struck the right balance between sophistication and the concept of the dining experience.

THE RUBY LOUNGE
The Ruby Lounge is the club and function space of the Eastern Hotel. Steeped in Chinese and Indian inspiration, a red illuminated bar runs the full length of the space. It was the intense red of the glowing bar that inspired the names "ruby" and "lounge."

THE BORDELLO
The Bordello is a red-curtained room with an expansive red leather bed and a mirrored ceiling. The room really couldn't have been called anything else!

THE DRAGON ROOM
The Dragon Room takes its name from the richly patterned dragon motifs embroidered onto the furniture.

PACIFICA
A terrace restaurant and bar occupies the fourth floor of the Eastern. The name "East Pacific" was originally proposed to link the Eastern and the Pacific Rim cuisine of the restaurant. The name was eventually shortened to Pacifica.

This dynamic and vibrant color system works because of its subconscious consistency. Although there is a unique color palette and concept around each corner, the designers have built-in elements, such as the typography and use of silver and gloss black, that unite the different areas of the hotel into a cohesive whole.

Using Art Deco motifs as a starting point, Layfield's designers created themes for each floor, uniting them with three common elements—typeface, color, and pattern.

TOP-SHELF STRATEGY

When Absolut was launched in 1979, its Swedish origins and iconic design brought simplicity, clarity, and perfection to the traditional vodka category. Fast forward twenty-five years and the brand needed to make the same impact on the emerging super-premium category, which is characterized by elaborately designed and highly embellished bottles.

The super-premium vodka, Absolut Level, is produced using a combination of continuous and batch distillation to give it a perfect balance of smoothness and character. Using "perfect balance" as the essence of the brief, the Pearlfisher design firm created a design for the new vodka's identity that elevated it to the super-premium category yet remained loyal to the overall Absolut brand.

The final design for the logo is a standout in the category that cleverly subverts the rules of premium vodka marketing. The tall bottle distinguishes Level from other Absolut vodkas and is a clear signal of its premium stature. However, the simple elegant design on frosted white glass is unique in a sector dominated by decoration. It is also distinctly Absolut.

By showing the name Level, Pearlfisher's designers were able to reflect the idea of "perfect balance," both visually and verbally. The name also implies that Absolut is reaching for a new level in the vodka beverage category. The name appears in a custom-created typeface and is accompanied by a silhouette of the iconic Absolut bottle, which succeeds in anchoring Level to the mother brand. The two elements work together to create a precise relationship between Absolut and Level, strengthening both brands; Level is endorsed by the well-known brand and Absolut is made more desirable by its foray into super-premium territory.

■ In order to distinguish Level from other Absolut vodkas, a taller frosted version of the iconic bottle was chosen to convey its premium stature.

CREATIVE DIRECTOR
SHAUN BOWEN

DESIGNER
NATALIE CHEUNG

CLIENT
VIN & SPRIT ABSOLUT SPIRITS

■ An array of clean, modern, and minimally embellished promotional items was designed to accompany Absolut Level's rollout and communicate the Absolut aesthetic. A custom typeface was created for the new product, which was paired with the traditional script found on their other products, further enhancing the Absolut brand.

:: Absolut Cut

A CUT ABOVE

Although a pioneering spirits brand, Absolut wasn't one
of the first vodkas to enter the premixed cocktail category.
Pearlfisher's LifeModes research highlighted an insurgence of
consumer modality—an increasing desire to mix up choices
and experiences. For example, consumers like to wear Gap
jeans with Jimmy Choo shoes or drink premium cocktails one
day and bottles of beer the next. With this in mind, Pearlfisher
LifeModes believed that Absolut had a lot to offer in the
premixed category.

Absolut and Pearlfisher LifeModes created Absolut Cut to
pioneer the next generation of premixed drinks. Its mission
was to elevate the status of the category by infusing it with
Absolut's quality and sophistication.

The name Cut was chosen because it best reflected the design
essence of "sophisticated edge." The word implies mixing
one drink with another (to cut with lime) and also signifies
a change in the company's direction. In addition, the short,
sharp nature of the word makes for a clear and snappy call
to the bartender—essential in a noisy bar environment.
To further communicate the name, the designers chose to
visualize the truth of the word "cut" by shaving off the edges
of the letters, which also mirrors the slashes in the bottle itself.

The Absolut brand has a great amount of equity, so
maintaining the iconic Absolut shape of the neck and
shoulders of the bottle was important. To differentiate it for
the new brand, the body of the bottle is randomly textured
with "cuts" in the glass. This reinforces the positioning of the
"sophisticated edge," since Cut is a harsher blend than the
smooth perfection of Absolut. The tactile nature of the bottle
also demonstrates to a first-time drinker that it's a hand-held
drink. The final product is a cool rendition of the timeless
brand and speaks effectively to this new target market.

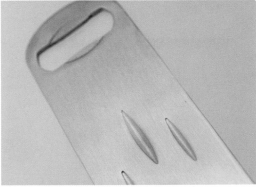

■ The simplicity of the Absolut Cut logo is a perfect
embellishment for promotional giveaways.

DESIGN FIRM
PEARLFISHER

CREATIVE DIRECTOR
SHAUN BOWEN

DESIGNER
LISA SIMPSON

CLIENT
VIN & SPRIT ABSOLUT SPIRITS

• The Absolut brand has a great amount of equity, so maintaining the iconic Absolut shape of the neck and shoulders of the bottle was important. But to differentiate it for the new brand, the body of the bottle is randomly textured with "cuts" in the glass.

A NEW BREED

A new type of salon was being launched in Edmonton, Alberta, whose founding partners envisioned a place where customers could be pampered but also could learn practical beauty secrets. They approached the WOW agency to develop a name and brand identity that would capture the essence of this concept.

The project was not fully funded when the design firm was approached, so WOW made a bold move and took the job anyway, telling the client that they would only have to pay if the project was financed. WOW's creatives believed that if the brand identity was complete, it would be easier for the partners to raise the needed money and, clearly, they were confident their work would make that a reality.

A STOLEN NAME

After heated creative battles, WOW's creatives selected the name "Perugia", the name of the man who stole the *Mona Lisa* from the Louvre Museum in 1911 and a region in Italy. The team loved the concept of "stolen beauty," plus the name had a pleasing yet unusual sound and a very desirable European aspect. The partners were thrilled.

THE BEAUTIFUL IDENTITY

One of the first concepts WOW explored included cool blue and green tones. While the imagery of clear water and pool tiles was calm and refreshing, this did not resonate well with the brand story. A warmer color system of layered orange tones, warm gray, and a light metallic gold was chosen instead. This new direction inspired concepts for the lush European interior space with terra-cotta textures and rich Italian stone details.

■ The founding partners of the Perugia Salon Spa envisioned a place where customers would be pampered but also could learn practical beauty secrets.

DESIGN FIRM
WOW BRANDING

CREATIVE DIRECTOR
PERRY CHUA

DESIGNERS
WILL JOHNSON, JEFF SCHRAMM

CLIENT
PERUGIA SALON SPA

- After heated creative battles, WOW's creatives selected the name "Perugia", the name of the man who stole the *Mona Lisa* from the Louvre Museum in 1911 and a region in Italy.

The ███ campaign for the Perugia Salon Spa captured the attention of ma██ ███radio and TV stations in Edmonton, Alberta. The high-profile event included a bikini art contest, a series of branded Mini automobiles, and mobile billboards.

The typeface in the Perugia Salon Spa logo was modified from an existing font that had the basic attributes (modern, sophisticated, and premium) WOW was looking for. Typography was kept contemporary to avoid too much of an Old World European feel.

The four-point star symbol in the logo represents the Perugia Salon Spa's commitment to unparalleled service and the promise of a rejuvenating experience for its guests.

■ Though the identity was inspired by Italian heritage, the brand needed to be perceived as hip and modern.
To incorporate these important qualities into the wordmark, WOW's designers used a typeface that
possessed the characteristics of a classic serif face and presented it in a clean and uncluttered fashion.

The four-point star symbol in the logo represents the salon's commitment to unparalleled service and the promise of a rejuvenating experience for its guests. The typeface in the logo was modified from an existing font that had the basic attributes (modern, sophisticated, and premium) WOW was looking for. The typography was kept contemporary to avoid too much of an Old World European feel. After all, the salon practiced traditional techniques with state-of-the-art equipment and technology.

A BRAVE LAUNCH
For the salon's launch, WOW's designers developed a grassroots campaign around art and beauty that would attract curious customers. Groups of fifty people dressed in orange wigs and T-shirts, some on stilts, paraded through the city of Edmonton holding signs with the salon's website address, "whatisbeauty.ca?" Handouts in the shape of a leaf were hung from tree branches downtown and given out on the streets, also including the "whatisbeauty.ca?" message. The website provided details about the salon and its opening day art contest, where six bikini-clad women were asked to create a unique piece of art—using only their bodies as a paintbrush.

Perugia Salon Spa is enjoying its exceptionally bold presence in the marketplace and is currently making plans to open more salons in North America.

REACHING OUT

Following the deregulation of the Italian telecommunications market in 1998, Tiscali initially established itself as a regional telephone operator and Internet service provider based in Cagliari, Italy. The company rapidly expanded throughout Italy, differentiating itself from its competitors with innovative services and marketing strategies. As of June 2004, Tiscali had 7.9 million active users, 1.44 million of whom were broadband customers, and the numbers continued to grow.

The name Tiscali refers to a 2,000-year-old nuragic village hidden in the center of Sardinia. For centuries, the village sheltered the Sardinian population from invaders' attacks, a shelter that provided protection because of its silence. Communication was born from the silence and communication supersedes isolation. From the land of silence and isolation, from a small island in the Mediterranean Sea, Tiscali broke the rules of monopoly and the name of the silent village became the name of a regional telecommunications provider that has developed into a pan-European company.

TISCALI'S NEW CALLING

As Tiscali grew as a company, the original logo, with typography and imagery inspired by the heritage of the region, seemed less appropriate for the global market. The new identity employs a modern visual language that's more fitting to Tiscali's growing international reputation. The logotype similarly reflects the technology-driven ethos of the brand and is accompanied by the new strapline, "Internet with a passion."

Designed by Pentagram partner Justus Oehler, the new identity system is currently being implemented across all relevant manifestations of the brand.

■ The new identity system for Tiscali, a regional telephone operator and Internet service provider based in Cagliari, Italy, is clean and sophisticated, while working seamlessly across a variety of applications.

DESIGN FIRM
PENTAGRAM DESIGN

CREATIVE DIRECTOR
JUSTUS OEHLER

DESIGNER
JUSTUS OEHLER

CLIENT
TISCALI

- As Tiscali grew as a company, the original logo, with typography and imagery inspired by the heritage of the region, seemed less appropriate for the global market. The new identity employs a modern visual language that's more fitting to Tiscali's growing international reputation.

:: Gas & Electric

THE ENLIGHTENING PROCESS

Gas & Electric is a television production company providing "visual energy" to the music and entertainment industry. The Atom design agency was approached by Gas & Electric to design a new identity for the company.

The client suggested a variety of new names, but they kept coming back to Gas & Electric. Working from this title, the chosen design comprised a main logo and various other symbols. The GE of the logo is loosely based on the heating elements of a pressure cooker, emphasizing the Gas & Electric name. The logo is broken down into an almost abstract mark, with the G as the E flipped, reflecting the unique perspectives of the two partners.

Alongside this logotype, the main symbol comprises a gas flame inside an electric bulb. With a name like Gas & Electric, light was the perfect creative platform, echoing the nature of film and television itself.

A BRIGHT IDENTITY

The clients wanted a design that reflected the origin of the name as a utility, so the designers pushed the envelope and based the look of the company's invoices on a gas or electricity bill. This concept was then applied to the business cards, which show the Gas & Electric bulb and logo on the front with a barcode on the reverse to add authenticity. The die-cut cards with rounded edges show a photograph of the employee as a young child treated with a very coarse halftone screen.

Additional icons created during the design process were used to create button badges. The strongest of these, showing a film camera projecting flames, is also used on the DVD show reel screen and cover.

■ Taking cues from this television production company's desire to be a "visual energy service provider," and with some inspiration from the Monopoly board game, the client chose the name Gas & Electric. To reinforce the utility company identity, business cards have the feel of employee ID cards, complete with a photo of the person as a child.

DESIGN FIRM
ATOM

CREATIVE DIRECTOR
JAMES BATES

DESIGNER
JAMES BATES

CLIENT
GAS & ELECTRIC

DESIGNING A MERGER

With the merger of two architecture firms, each with its own existing equity, the newly formed company needed a totally new identity. The catch? Only the principals of CDFM2 and Heinlein Schrock Stearns knew of the merger, so the deal needed to be kept confidential until it was officially released. The solution was to conduct secret naming and brand strategy meetings at the Design Ranch identity firm.

The challenge was to find common ground among the eight partners, knowing that each partner preferred to have his or her name or initials on the door. Design Ranch's mission was twofold: to differentiate this company from the partner-naming practice present in every architecture firm in the country and to create a name that all the partners would embrace. The new brand had to reflect each firm's independent histories, while also symbolizing the potential of their shared future. Plus, the identity had to communicate the new firm's design expertise and the full range of services.

Because of the legal urgency of the merger, the naming process, brand identity design, and printing had to be completed in just five weeks. With a timeline this tight, quick decisions had to be made. The partners agreed to separate into committees to expedite the decision-making process, intending for each decision maker to narrow down the field to a final presentation that all the partners could agree upon.

Even though Design Ranch compiled a list of more than 200 names, one name stood apart from the rest and exemplified all aspects of the new firm. Thus, 360° Architecture was born.

Fittingly, a circle became the grounding shape for the logo; the typography was drafted with soft edges, reflective of the circle that bled off the sides, creating a global, 360-degree experience. To reinforce the excitement, strength, and energy

■ Sketches, drafting, blueprints, and photography from two merging firms were collaged together to create an oversized poster, highlighting the creativity of each firm and the new shared vision. The poster was printed and trimmed down to make over 100 business cards, giving each employee a different back to their card. At the announcement party, the cards were distributed and each staff member posted their own card to the wall to re-create the poster.

DESIGN FIRM
DESIGN RANCH

CREATIVE DIRECTORS
MICHELLE SONDEREGGER, INGRED SIDIE

DESIGNERS
TAD CARPENTER, RACHEL KARACA

CLIENT
360° ARCHITECTURE

• Even though Design Ranch compiled a list of more than 200 possible brand names, one name stood apart from the rest and exemplified all aspects of the new firm. Thus, 360° Architecture was born.

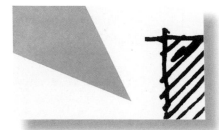

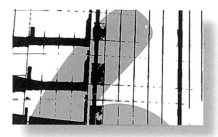

THREESIXTY ARCHITECTURE

360°

GEORGE HEINLEIN, AIA PRINCIPAL

1015 CENTRAL STREET   T. 816.472.2000
KANSAS CITY MO 64105   F. 816.471.4362

1801 MCGEE SUITE 200   T. 816.531.3003
KANSAS CITY MO 64108   F. 816.531.3388

E. GHEIN@360ARCHITECTS.COM

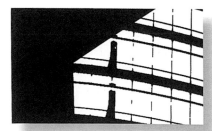

■ At the announcement party for the new firm, each employee was given a keepsake minibook that highlighted the individuals from both firms with a photograph and brief biography of each.

of the new firm, red was a natural choice for the predominant color, further strengthening the mark.

When developing the collateral materials, Design Ranch obtained sketches, drafting, blueprints, and photography from both firms and collaged them together to create an oversized poster highlighting the creativity of each firm and their new-shared vision. The poster was printed and trimmed down to make over 100 business cards, giving each employee a different back for their own card.

BUILDING AWARENESS

The business cards were distributed at a companywide announcement party and each staff member posted his or her card on the wall to re-create the poster. As employees added their pieces to the puzzle, it was a team-building exercise that also created a stunning visual collage as a centerpiece to the party. Introductions were made and a shared camaraderie was instilled, laying the groundwork for an exciting future. A keepsake minibook was given to each employee that highlighted the individuals from both firms with a photograph and brief biography of each.

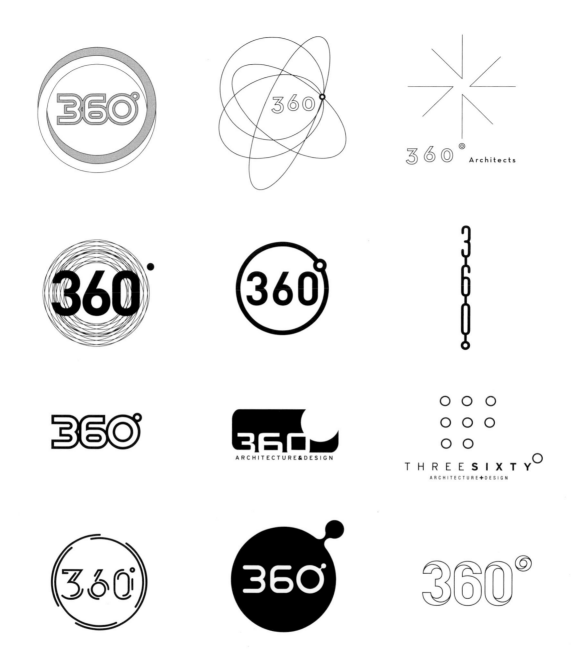

■ Fittingly, a circle became the grounding shape for the logo; and the typography was drafted with soft edges, reflective of the circle, that bled off the sides, creating a global, 360-degree experience.

∷ Mestisos

MAN'S BEST CONCEPT

Located in Vancouver, British Columbia, Mestisos Pet Spa is the city's most luxurious spa for dogs. It is a state-of-the-art facility that provides the ultimate in pampering for pets.

Mestisos was the inspiration of two brothers whose passion was breeding and showing champion bloodline boxers. After years spent at the most glamorous dog shows in North America, they began to envision a spa where all dogs could be treated like show champions, no matter what their lineage.

When the brothers approached the Blu Concept design agency, they focused on their core values, their stories from the dog show circuit, and most importantly, their vision. From these initial discussions, the direction for the entire brand was apparent.

Literally translated, the word "mestisos" means "mixed ancestry," a name that seemed integral to their brand philosophy. Their vision was to create a dog spa that catered to all dogs, not just the purebred and privileged. Every dog would be treated to the exclusive Mestisos experience. The firm's challenge was to crystallize the client's vision in a tangible way that could be articulated and embraced by their clients.

GROOMING THE CONCEPT

First, the team identified everything they didn't want Mestisos to be. From their years in the canine community, the Villafuerte brothers had plenty of experience with groomers and breeders to draw from. Mestisos needed to be clean, elegant, and above all, professional. They wanted it to have similar attributes as a sophisticated spa for people, except with a definite dog personality.

For Mestisos Pet Spa, the designers envisioned colors that were soothing and refined but, at the same time, upscale and dramatic. After trying several color combinations, they settled on a palette that reflected the symbolism of the

■ Blu Concept's designers created multiple versions of Mestisos Pet Spa's business cards. The rounded corners gave a softened touch in contrast to the masculine color palette.

Mestisos name. Equal proportions of clean white and pure black were seen together and then mixed to create a perfectly balanced, harmonious gray. This aesthetic was not limited to the identity but was carried through to the spa itself. Black awnings, polished gray etched-concrete floors, white walls, and black ironwork accents helped define the Mestisos experience. In addition to the balance of the core identity, the designers added fresh transparent tones, such as hues of

DESIGN FIRM
BLU CONCEPT INC.

CREATIVE DIRECTOR
RICHARD KLINGLE-WATT

DESIGNER
JENA POWELL

CLIENT
MESTISOS PET SPA

PET SPA
iSOS

Massage Therapy
Custom Sized Treadmills
Aromatherapy
Self Wash Stations
Educational Seminars
Breed Rescue Weekends
Breeder Referral
Home Delivery Services
Pick-Up & Drop-Off Services

3087 Oak Street Vancouver (Oak & 15th)   604.738.0033   www.mestisos.com

Hydrotherapy
Grooming
Fine Products

Spa services for dogs.

■ Since Blu Concept's designers were dealing with such a strict set of components, they felt they could maintain and even evolve the brand identity through manipulation of the core elements. As a result, multiple versions of the business cards were created, each very distinctive, but all still true to the original vision.

glass, to soften the tones of the brochure and postcards, yet maintain the dramatic feel.

With the tone and palette in place, Blu Concept's designers set about creating the identity, which happened very naturally. They felt the name was so original and memorable that they decided to make that center stage and have the dog icon play a secondary role. For the image, they chose a silhouette of a

proud boxer, which both paid homage to the brothers' breeding heritage and provided the perfect statement for the spa.

The overall look achieved just the level of sophistication and elegance the client had originally outlined and clearly speaks to those seeking a high-quality experience for their own four-legged champions, whether they have papers or not.

:: Wax Branded

WAX ON

Wax is a small, trend-savvy marketing firm. Bamboo liked the name Wax Branded because not only is it fresh and quick, it's also unique among competing marketing firms. As a word, wax also holds multiple, relevant meanings. Wax can mean, "to become" something (e.g., wax rhapsodic) and as a firm, Wax is dedicated to adopting and developing a brand. Wax is also pliable, relating to how the firm essentially molds the client's brand into what they want it to be. Finally, it indicates a clean, slick, polished result, the desirable effect after a branding initiative.

HIGH-GLOSS DESIGN

Bamboo first brainstormed thematic ideas relating to the brand positioning, then created possible names within those themes. Any names that were to be presented needed to pass a preliminary trademark search to ensure the name was available. For Wax Branded, they created rough visual designs and presented the client with just a few of their favorites from the long list of possibilities. With some clients, a visual association with the name helps bring the brand to life.

The client decided rather quickly to go with Wax Branded because it so perfectly reflected the important values of the firm: flexibility, a personal touch, and sleek, intelligent branding. Rather than using a logomark, which can become dated over time, the team designed the Wax Branded wordmark with the intention that it would almost always be accompanied by additional graphic elements. This allows for growth and flexibility within the system, an ideal setup for a branding company. The color is energetic, vibrant, and speaks to the company's personality. The floral motif represents a fresh perspective and perpetual adaptation to new situations and challenges. Overall, the system is modern, and fresh, but professional, and savvy.

■ The Bamboo design firm designed the Wax Branded word-mark intending for it to almost always be accompanied by additional graphic elements, allowing for growth and flexibility. The color is energetic, vibrant, and speaks to the company's personality. The floral motif represents a fresh perspective and perpetual adaptation to new situations and challenges. The overall identity was designed to look modern and fresh but professional and savvy.

DESIGN FIRM
BAMBOO

CREATIVE DIRECTOR
KATHY SORANNO

DESIGNER
KATHY SORANNO

CLIENT
DARCIE PURCELL

• The client decided rather quickly to go with the name Wax Branded for its marketing company because it so perfectly reflected the important values of the firm: flexibility, a personal touch, and sleek, intelligent branding.

■ The very complex branding project for Eos Airlines included creating designs for everything from airplane livery, pillows, and blankets to their website, trade show space, onboard collateral, and airport signage.

TAKING OFF

Hornall Anderson Design Works (HADW) was enlisted by New York-based Eos Airlines to design an entire branding program for their daily roundtrip transatlantic service. Eos provides its passengers with personal space by placing forty-eight seats on the same size plane that usually accommodates over 200 seats. This premium-class service targets the discerning traveler, offering the comfort of suites, not seats.

A SOARING SCOPE

Included in this all-encompassing and very complex branding project was the company's vision planning, corporate brand strategy (which identified everything from a clear market positioning to service behaviors), naming, logo, identity, and airplane graphics. HADW was there from start to finish, designing the aircraft's exterior livery as well as its interior branded elements: throw pillows, headrests, sleep program (lamb's wool/cashmere blankets, sleep pillows, amenity kits), flight attendant uniforms, aircraft signage placards, corporate business papers, website design (www.eosairlines. com), messaging, and product name strategy, trade show graphics, collateral materials on board the aircraft signage, airport gate signage, and press kit design.

DESIGN FIRM
HORNALL ANDERSON DESIGN WORKS

CREATIVE DIRECTOR
JACK ANDERSON

DESIGNERS
LINDA HALVERSON, LAURA JAKOBSEN, MARK POPICH, DAVID BATES, ANDREW WICKLUND, LEO RAYMUNDO, JACOB CARTER, YURI SHVETS, LARRY ANDERSON

CLIENT
EOS AIRLINES

Named after the Greek goddess of dawn, Eos provides its passengers with personal space by placing forty-eight seats on the same size plane that usually accommodates over 200 seats. This premium-class service targets the discerning traveler, offering the comfort of suites, not seats.

■ Included in this all-encompassing project was the company's vision planning, corporate brand strategy (which identified everything from a clear market positioning to service behaviors), naming, logo, identity, and airplane graphics.

Focusing on the key attributes of sophisticated, perceptive, confident, and human, the design team created a premium aesthetic that speaks to Eos Airlines' overall messaging and style. Artistic impression is reflected in the Eos identity, illustrated with a featherlike mark accenting the letter O and hinting at flight and comfort, in addition to indicating the long O pronunciation. Named for the Greek goddess of dawn, Eos Airlines' color palette of blue and gold was chosen to reflect the idea of the morning sky with the gold accent mark representing a sunrise.

THE LANDING

The ultimate goal of Eos Airlines was to focus on the joy of traveling from the moment its passengers leave for the airport. They were striving to make it personal—delivering the first truly customer-centric experience to the premium airlines market. Because HADW focused on important details such as blankets and premium food, Eos Airlines is able to give its passengers a calming and comfortable atmosphere—a place tailored to whatever world-class business travelers need to revive, rejuvenate, and relax.

N546US

BOEING 757-200

eos

eos

The featherlike mark accenting the letter O hints at the notions of flight and comfort, as well as the correct long O pronunciation.

Origin

Names that are rooted in origin generally pay tribute to the founders or the inspirational place from which the brand was born. These names can be real and or fictitious but are always rooted in meaning. Famous examples include Dell, Bartles and James, and New York Fries.

THEIR NAME IS EARLS

The "Earls" in Earls Restaurant pays homage to the middle names of its founder, Leroy Earl Fuller, and his son, President Stanley Earl Fuller. The Fullers shared a love for food and conversation, so entering the restaurant industry was a perfect fit. In 1982, the first Earls opened in Edmonton, Alberta, Canada. Over twenty years later, there are now fifty Earls throughout Western Canada, Arizona, and Colorado. At the root of their success are the Fuller family's genuine passion for the business of hospitality and a knack for knowing what their customers want.

THE BRAND FAMILY VALUES

Earls Restaurants helped define the casual dining industry over twenty years ago by bridging the gap between fast food and fine dining. Earls caters to a broad clientele, but over the years they lost their leadership position as the onset of trendy competitors began hooking a younger audience. By revitalizing the existing identity and brand image, Earls hoped to attract a hipper crowd. Earls needed to provide more than just great food and great service. It also had to be seen as a place where life was good and where customers could nourish their souls *and* their bellies.

Karacters' key insight was to create a modern, sophisticated, experiential journey for customers, and one that would connect with them on an emotional level.

A DELICIOUS PROCESS

Earls did not want to stray too far from their original Bembo typeface wordmark. The "e" imprint on their existing flatware was valuable to the brand, plus they wanted to keep using it, so Karacters explored typefaces that were similar to Bembo and decided a visual mark would be used to add personality. Karacters explored illustration styles and felt a logo drawn in one continuous line would best tell the story. The final

■ The inspiration for Earls' logo redesign was to capture the true spirit of a place to experience great food and great company. A martini glass morphs into the shape of a woman's mouth, which is intertwined with a man's smiling face, representing Earls as not just a restaurant but as a gathering place where people can have a drink and socialize.

■ The large, playful images of people enjoying food and friends communicate the social spirit of Earls Restaurants.

DESIGN FIRM
KARACTERS DESIGN GROUP

CREATIVE DIRECTOR
JAMES BATEMAN

DESIGNERS
NANCY WU, MARSHA LARKIN, KARA BOHL

CLIENT
EARLS RESTAURANT

Earls needed to provide more than just great food and great service. It also had to be seen as a place where life was good and where customers could nourish their souls *and* their bellies.

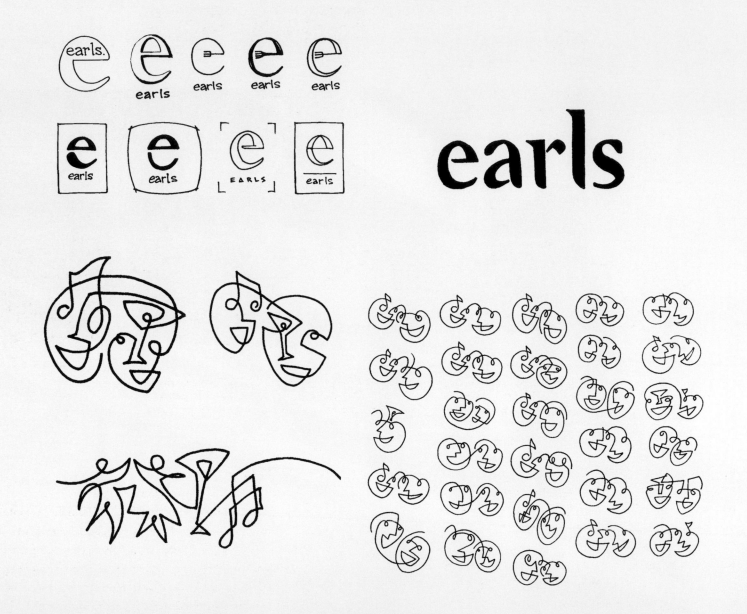

earls

Karacters' designers decided a visual mark would be used to add personality to the brand. Karacters explored illustration styles and felt a logo drawn in one continuous line would best tell the story.

■ The orange, red, hot pink, and yellow color combination was chosen to express the warm, friendly spirit found at Earls and is used on all pieces of collateral. The large-scale images of attractive young people actively and happily eating and drinking make it impossible to ignore the emotional connection between people and food.

illustration was composed of just three lines of varying weights to make it visually interesting without looking too perfect; a thorough linear study of the entwined faces with the martini glass ensured legibility and balance.

Karacters created a custom, hand-rendered wordmark based on a combination of different typefaces, including Bembo, to give the logo a fresh and contemporary look. This iconic device was designed to reinforce the sociable spirit of the brand, with the two intercepting faces representing people coming together, engaging in conversation. The logo now epitomizes the energy and spirit of the brand, bringing the social atmosphere to life.

ALL TOGETHER NOW

In addition to the logo, Karacters developed a new creative platform for Earls that celebrated the idea of "bringing people together." The emotive values that captured Earls' sociability were infused into the identity and carried through on all pieces of collateral. Vibrant photographic images of people enjoying food with their friends celebrated Earls' atmosphere as a social catalyst. The entwined faces of the logo were also overlaid to create a pattern used as a secondary graphic device. This repeating image emphasizes the friendly, high-energy dining environment—the essence of the Earls Restaurant brand.

THE DRIVER FOR REBRANDING

DentonWildeSapte, a top ten UK law firm employing 1,700 people, aimed to reposition itself as a firm focused on four key industry sectors. DentonWildeSapte felt that too many law firms pretended to offer a full range of services in all sectors when they only had strengths in a few. DentonWildeSapte wanted to make a virtue out of its clarity of focus.

The challenge was to make this strategy sound like a progressive choice for both the marketplace and the firm itself. They were concerned that saying they were focused on only four industry sectors could easily be seen as narrow and unappealing.

SOLVING THE PUZZLE

Salterbaxter's design strategy gets to the heart of the rationale behind DentonWildeSapte's business plan. It's all about positioning the firm as the knowledge leader in its chosen sectors.

To achieve this, the brand story was based on the concept of knowledge, using a strapline (A strapline is an advertising slogan attached to a brand name to emphasize a phrase that the company wishes to be remembered for.) "It's a knowledge thing.... " The lawyers were initially nervous using the word "knowledge" because they didn't want to be seen as know-it-alls. By turning the line upside down, it provides a more intuitive way of explaining the idea. This solution ensures that the emphasis is placed on "knowledge that solves problems" rather than just "knowledge."

Initially, the law firm said things like, "We've heard it all before—a firm will go through a rebrand and just change the shade of blue—they'll lose their nerve." The managing board, vowed to choose a color that was bold, striking, and noticeable—even if people were uncomfortable with it. And so, fluorescent red was chosen.

■ The strapline, "It's a knowledge thing...," was designed to focus on the firm's brand promise: "knowledge that solves problems." The strapline has been turned upside down to mimic the look of a quiz book, with a question at the top and the answer upside down at the bottom, thus illustrating the idea that knowledge solves problems.

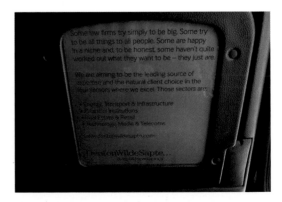

■ The DentonWildeSapte law firm hired Salterbaxter to reposition its focus on only four key industry sectors, emphasizing the firm's strengths rather than spreading itself too thin by offering a full range of services. They chose to turn their clarity of focus into a virtue.

DESIGN FIRM
SALTERBAXTER

CLIENT
DENTONWILDESAPTE

International lawyers

DentonWildeSapte...

it's a knowledge thing

bright thinking

www.dentonwildesapte.com

• During the early research for the project, the law firm's principals said things like, "We've heard it all before—a firm will go through a rebrand and just change the shade of blue—they'll lose their nerve."

◆◆ Huairasinchi

THE STRENGTH OF A NAME

After the successful inauguration of their adventure race in Ecuador, the organizers of Huairasinchi debated whether or not they needed to have a more commercial name. Because the race's original Ecuadorian name, Huairasinchi, had a valuable meaning —"the strength of the wind"—Giotto Design chose to keep the name rather than find a more commercial one.

Using concepts from the native culture where the race originated, Giotto Design decided to create a new logo that would better reflect the philosophy of the race—constant movement. The team also paid special attention to how the logo would work when applied to the wide range of marketing collateral.

It was a risk to develop a name in the Quechua language, especially because many in Ecuadorian society had moved away from their cultural heritage. But the mix of aboriginal and contemporary styles in the race's logo and corporate image was a winning combination for reaching the public. Infused with new life, the Huairasinchi brand lured more than 500 national and international registrants to compete in the next year's race.

The marketing collateral uses vibrant colors and photography of adventure sports. All race participant materials also include the color and photo system to entice potential registrants by showing the most striking landscapes and landmarks of Ecuador's backcountry.

To achieve their goal of becoming one of the top three adventure races in South America, Huirasinchi has consequently invested in a comprehensive marketing plan including a website, video, and promotion campaign.

■ For the Huairasinchi adventure race logo, the designers chose to incorporate both aboriginal and contemporary styles to reflect the philosophy of the race while giving it a fresh look.

■ The marketing collateral and race participant materials include vibrant color and adventure sport photos to entice potential registrants. Each piece showcases the most striking landscapes and landmarks of Ecuador's back-country as further incentive to participate in the race.

DESIGN FIRM
GIOTTO DESIGN

CREATIVE DIRECTOR
SILVIO GIORGI

DESIGNERS
SILVIO GIORGI, SANDRO GIORGI

CLIENT
HUAIRASINCHI

HUAIRASINCHI

COMPETENCIA DE AVENTURA

- Because the race's original Ecuadorian name, Huairasinchi, had a valuable meaning —"the strength of the wind"— Giotto Design chose to keep the name rather than find a more commercial one.

STARTING ON HUBBARD STREET

Since Liska designed its first logo in 1978, they've been intimately involved with building and evolving the Hubbard Street Dance Chicago (HSDC) brand. As HSDC has achieved worldwide acclaim, Liska established a branding system for promoting their performances internationally, which can be understood in any country where the dance company appears. The branding system is a Web-based guideline that includes history, color palettes, typography, style guides, templates, and examples of materials such as posters, ads, etc. They also upload new dance images every six months to ensure that promoters use the most up-to-date imagery. Hubbard Street has no visual control over promoters and local venues usually do what they want in terms of marketing, but almost every time they received a performance poster from Berlin or New York, it looked like Liska + Associates designed it. And the promoters were thrilled to have guidelines, examples, and assets to work with.

More than twenty-five years ago, the Hubbard Street Dance Company was founded when choreographer Lou Conte and four dancers gave free performances in various locations around Chicago. Named for the studio's first location in Chicago at Hubbard Street and LaSalle Street, "Hubbard" evoked a gritty, urban neighborhood in downtown Chicago. Liska created the company's first logo, which focused on the word "dance" because few dance groups existed in Chicago at the time. It also reflected the Broadway-influenced performances that the original company was known for.

BUILDING HOMETOWN AWARENESS

By its fifteenth year, the dance company had grown exponentially, performing both internationally and nationally from Poland to the Netherlands to Montana. Taking these changes into consideration, Liska helped HSDC redesign its logo. This time, the name changed from "Company" to "Chicago" to

- Liska designed the first HSDC logo in 1978 and has since partnered with them as their exclusive design firm. As HSDC grew both in size and reputation, the logo and brand identity changed several times. At one point, the name changed from Company to Chicago to make the connection with its hometown, building awareness as it traveled the globe. The first iteration featured "Co." at the bottom, the second incorporated horizontal bars, and the current mark uses only the icon and the type.

DESIGN FIRM
LISKA + ASSOCIATES

CREATIVE DIRECTOR
STEVE LISKA

DESIGNERS
LOGO: STEVE LISKA, WEB: SABINE KRAUSS, BANNERS: CAROLE MASSE

CLIENT
HUBBARD STREET DANCE CHICAGO

**HUBBARD
STREET
DANCE
CHICAGO**

ANNUAL REPORT 2003

▪ No name change was needed for the twenty-fifth anniversary of the HSDC, but the logo needed to visually reflect the personality of the company at that time—bold, sensual, and sophisticated. The current logo represents the dual forces of structure and flexibility that are evident in the achievements of this world-class dance company.

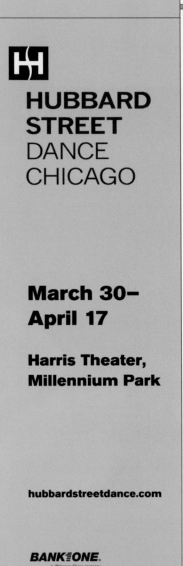

Once Liska designed new brand materials, they needed to make them available to the various promoters around the world who bring the HSDC to their cities. They developed an intuitive, Web-based program for distributing HSDC marketing materials anywhere in the world.

■ To prevent international promoters from creating inconsistent marketing materials, Liska developed a branding system for HSDC to promote its performances worldwide, which is now easily recognizable in any country where the dance company appears. The branding system is a Web-based guideline that includes history, color palettes, typography, style guides, templates, and examples of materials such as posters, ads, etc.

make the connection between the troupe and its hometown, building awareness as it traveled the globe. The emphasis in the logo was still on dance, although it incorporated the Chicago element of the new name.

THE NEW HUBBARD STREET

No name change was needed for the twenty-fifth anniversary, but the logo needed to visually reflect the personality of the company at that time—bold, sensual, and sophisticated. The current logo represents the dual forces of structure and flexibility that are evident in the achievements of this world-class dance company.

Once Liska designed new brand materials, they needed to make them available to the various promoters around the world who bring HSDC to their cities. In the past, promoters had created their own marketing materials, which were inconsistent with the HSDC brand and contributed to the public's confusion. To protect and promote the brand more effectively, Liska developed an intuitive, Web-based program for distributing HSDC marketing materials anywhere in the world. The result has been consistent promotional materials that all look and feel part of the HSDC brand family.

A NEW FOCUS

SEA was approached in 2001 to create an identity for a new
office furniture business founded by Richmond Solutions,
a successful company that sold furniture from various
manufacturers. Martin Scofield, CEO of Richmond Solutions,
wanted to completely change his business model—and not
merely with a rebrand or a rename. To compete with rising
industry leaders, he began designing and manufacturing
his own line of high-specification office furniture. Scofield
collaborated with SEA on all elements of the identity
development to launch Richmond Solutions' design-centric
business called beyon.

The name *beyon*, taken from one designer's surname, was
chosen as the company name. The name works on several
levels: the b of beyon is almost like a stamp of approval that
can brand the products; its simple lines are as graceful as the
furniture; and it evokes chairs, seating, and modern work
spaces. The mark is also very visually fluid—reflecting the
beyon furniture itself.

To accurately communicate the personality of the product
line, SEA chose each element carefully. The subtler mark
always appears in either in white, gray, or black, while the
colors of the other elements are striking and bold. The
dynamic color palette is then offset by typography that is clean
and confident, allowing the highly visual imagery to remain
center stage. SEA then developed brand guidelines that clearly
outline the logotype, typeface, color palette, tone of voice, and
use of imagery, ensuring their vision is always delivered in a
consistent manner.

SELLING THE IDEA

The new company needed to launch their products, brand,
and identity to architects who would be sourcing beyon's

■ The simple and modern lines of the beyon logo echo
the high-end furniture the brand is now known for.
This sensibility is carried throughout its advertising
campaign and across all collateral materials.

DESIGN FIRM
SEA

CREATIVE DIRECTORS
BRYAN EDMONDSON, JOHN SIMPSON

DESIGNER
STUART L. BAILEY

CLIENT
BEYON

• Martin Scofield, CEO of Richmond Solutions, wanted to completely change his business model—and not merely with a rebrand or a rename. To compete with rising industry leaders, he began designing and manufacturing his own line of high-specification office furniture.

beyon™
Confidence at work

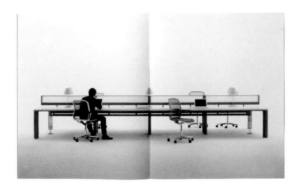

■ The beyon philosophy is to create working environments that are open and inviting, inspirational and motivational.
The clean and contemporary furniture is essentially modern with classic substance and beauty.

furniture for their projects. The shoot for the launch took place overnight in the Tate Modern Museum in London, a venue instantly recognizable to the architects beyon wanted to target. A subsequent campaign was photographed at London's City Airport, a small airport in East London used mostly for European and national flights, another iconic design location and one that emphasizes the business market beyon is targeting. Both locations created stunning backdrops, while adding drama to the imagery. These images were used in a high impact, above-the-line billboard campaign across the UK and in Sydney, Australia.

The cool minimalism of the identity and sleek product brochures were created to appeal to a design-savvy audience. To further entice this audience, they incorporated

unique materials and finishes. The designers were able to communicate the quality of the product on a subconscious level by foiling and embossing the logo to emphasize the "stamp" of the mark on the literature and using paper stocks such as heavy board or case bindings with a substantial feel to emphasize the solidity of the furniture.

At the end of the day, beyon has not only tapped its target architect audience but they have also won many awards for their beautifully designed furniture.

· The cool minimalism of the identity and sleek product brochures were created to appeal to a design-savvy audience.

Playful

Names that are fun, high-spirited, and challenge the ordinary—they generally make you smile. This style of name is not specific to any industry but certainly reflects a company's personality. Famous examples include Yahoo and Guess.

THE STRATEGY IS "FUN"

Pocoyo is an animated television series for preschool children that follows the main character Pocoyo and his friends on whimsical yet educational adventures. Aware of research that showed children could learn at least 15 percent more when the learning is made into a fun experience, the creators based *Pocoyo's* strategy on the tag line, "Learning through Laughter." *Pocoyo* combined the delivery of information with entertainment to achieve the goal of educating children more effectively; that is the key to differentiating their brand.

AN INSPIRED NAME

The story behind the name Pocoyo comes from the daughter of David Cantolla, the cocreator of the *Pocoyo* television series. Two-year-old Vega would say the following prayer in Spanish: "Jesusito de mi vida tu eres niño como yo," which translates into "Baby Jesus, light of my life, you are a child like me." Instead of saying "como yo" at the end of the prayer, she mistakenly said "poco yo." Her father thought her funny phrase would make a great name for the television series and others at the company agreed. While "poco yo" isn't a real word or phrase, its closest interpretation in Spanish is "little me." This concept couldn't be more fitting for the eponymous star of the show, a young yet self-aware little boy.

SIMPLIFYING THE IDENTITY PROCESS

Before the team at Zinkia created the *Pocoyo* brand, they agreed on the following criteria to shape the overall vision for the series:

- Simple yet expressive characters, each with a strong and well-defined personality
- Real characters, not the typical preschool stereotype
- A series based on humor but with a strong educational base
- A vibrant color system without any distracting backgrounds
- A simple but interesting musical score that both children and parents would enjoy

■ Because certain products can only be produced in a limited range of colors, several versions of the logo had to be developed to cover various product uses.

DESIGN FIRM
ZINKIA ENTERTAINMENT

CREATIVE DIRECTORS
DAVID CANTOLLA, GUILLERMO GARCIA, LUIS GALLEGO

DESIGNERS
DANIEL SANLLEHI, OSCAR GARCIA

CLIENT
GRANADA VENTURES

- The building blocks of the Pocoyo logo are colorful and cartoonlike to appeal to their young audience but parents recognize it as an educational tool.

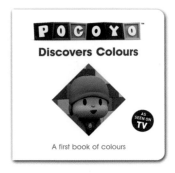

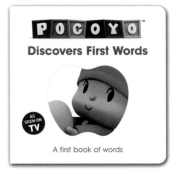

▪ Knowing that clean designs and bright, contrasting colors can improve a child's ability to concentrate and can stimulate his learning development, the illustrations in the spin-off books from the children's educational series, *Pocoyo*, were even more minimalist than the television images.

Zinkia's research showed that a minimalist style and clean design could actually help children to concentrate. Additionally, bright colors in contrasting shades could help stimulate development. Even though children can see color from birth, very young children have difficulty distinguishing different tones such as red from orange. Therefore, contrasting colors are important when designing for this market. As children develop the ability to distinguish shades, they prefer primary colors, which the *Pocoyo* team used to their advantage.

Their logo, multicolored building blocks that spell out POCOYO, follows the minimalist mode and is the basis for the way information is presented on the show. Early-learning concepts, such as numbers, shapes, colors, and patterns, are introduced in a clear, simple manner but in a vivid and imaginative presentation.

A final crucial factor for a brand whose audience is too young to actually procure the product for themselves, *Pocoyo* needed to appeal to preschoolers as well as adults. In order for the brand to succeed, parents had to feel it offered trustworthy products that they would want their children to enjoy. For example, the building blocks logo is colorful and cartoonlike to appeal to their young audience but parents recognize it as an educational tool similar to those they may have previously bought for their children or remember playing with themselves when they were children.

A limited color palette and a focus on clean, simple lines were used to design the characters, thereby removing all extraneous visual flourishes and helping children concentrate on better understanding each character's personality.

Aware of research that showed children could learn at least 15 percent more when the learning is made into a fun experience, the creators based Pocoyo's strategy on the tag line, "Learning through Laughter."

CHARACTER DEVELOPMENT

After the brand's identity was determined, the team created a unique look and feel for *Pocoyo's* characters by incorporating the novel combination of a minimalist style with strong visual wit. The identity works well not only within the context of the program but also across a wide range of *Pocoyo* products, giving it a distinct look in the children's market. A limited color palette and a focus on clean, simple lines were used to design the characters, thereby removing all extraneous visual flourishes and helping children concentrate on better understanding each character's personality.

Pocoyo's look was partially inspired by traditional Japanese anime characters, a passion of Cantolla and his creative colleague, Guillermo Garcia. Inspired by these designs that are developed with a global illumination technique, one of the first ideas for *Pocoyo* was to contrast the appeal of a cute little boy with the confidence and determination that kids are also well known for. Global illumination is a technique used to give the object or character a tactile, sensory, and cute appearance. It adds texture and makes the viewer want to reach out and touch the image as though it were a plush toy or clay object. The technique gives the impression of light coming from different angles rather than from just one light source.

Pocoyo was also given a more realistic look than many animated characters by providing him with a variety of comical expressions. He wears a hat that covers his eyebrows instead of the typical cartoon image of high-arched eyebrows with wide-open eyes.

Pocoyo is now a recognizable brand for children in sixty countries that can be found on a wide range of products including books, plush toys, children's clothing, bedding, tableware, posters, and flatware.

In *Pocoyo*, an animated children's television series, the main character and his friends are delighted with discovering everyday objects. It encourages children to do the same when exploring their own world.

  **Shirts for people.**

SACK™   Home   All T-Shirts   Order FAQ   Contact   Links   Mail List   Affiliate   Log In   Your Sack

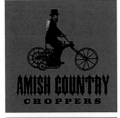   

■ The Sack brand name and logo were inspired by the traditional clothing styles known as sack suits and sack dresses that were popular in the early twentieth century. The website uses a range of both traditional and nontraditional images to attract customers seeking an alternative online shopping destination.

UNCONVENTIONAL INSPIRATION

Ad agency 3 decided to launch its own T-shirt site as a fun, creative outlet as well as a unique profit-making opportunity. They envisioned that the website would appeal to people who typically avoided buying apparel from mainstream retailers and instead sought out alternative choices. The name of the website had to clearly reflect the attitude, humor, and design of the T-shirts they were selling but it was also important that the logo wasn't overly designed or slick. To support this strategy, they developed a theme around rejecting the conservative corporate world, an ideology that would resonate with their target audience.

WRAPPING THEIR HEADS AROUND IT

The creative team decided to invent an original slang word for "T-shirt." "Wrapper," "baggage," and "shell" each conveyed the authentic, rebellious nature of the brand, but none of them sounded as original or memorable as "sack."

DESIGN FIRM
3

CREATIVE DIRECTOR
SAM MACLAY

DESIGNER
TIM MCGRATH

CLIENT
SACK

CUSTOMER 1045

COMMA SUTRA T SHIRT

Comma Sutra

SACK™
www.sackwear.com

SACKWEAR.COM

Probably the web's funniest t-shirts.

• The Sack brand embodies the attitudes of rebellion: making a statement, looking unique, and the desire to be perceived as outrageous. The brand had to appeal to those who've bucked the status quo and feel comfortable making a statement with their clothing choices, however unusual or irreverent.

SACK™

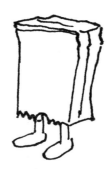

■ The name of the Sackwear.com website had to clearly reflect the attitude, humor, and design of the T-shirts they were selling but it was also important that the logo wasn't overly designed or slick. To support this strategy, they developed a theme around rejecting the conservative corporate world, an ideology that would resonate with their target audience.

■ The combination of unusual images and witty quips that are printed on their T-shirts humorously differentiates Sackwear.com's products from other T-shirt sources found on the Web.

On a secondary level, sack also suggests shopping, a perfect tie-in with e-commerce. With the name in place, they chose the URL sackwear.com because they wanted the brand to be able to eventually expand their product line beyond T-shirts into a brand that encompasses a whole attitude.

Once the name and URL were determined, the logo quickly followed. With imagery stemming from the ideas the name suggested—a sack one could wear and the idea of traditional, conservative apparel— the image of a man in a business suit with the bag on his head became an ideal mark.

The brand embodies the attitudes of rebellion: making a statement, looking unique, and the desire to be perceived as outrageous. The Sack name and logo wholeheartedly support this in a fresh way that appeals to those who've bucked the status quo and feel comfortable making a statement with their clothing choices, however unusual or irreverent.

A CATTY CONCEPT

In the cutthroat competitivity of alcoholic beverages, established brands can provide positive name recognition by introducing a new product to a crowded shelf. But for that new product to succeed, it still must build its own brand equity by uniquely connecting with the consumer separate from the "mother" brand.

Sour Puss is a successful brand of liqueur typically used for mixing martinis and shooters. Developing a ready-to-drink (RTD) beverage, allowed Sour Puss to expand into a different category—but it also needed a different brand identity, so the RTD wouldn't cannibalize its core audience.

Dossier took a unique approach that created a distinct and attractive personality for the new product, effectively catapulting it into the RTD market. Although they took some cues from Sour Puss—they focused on the same target audience of socially conscious men and women in their twenties and used a cat as an icon—they were able to distinguish it by choosing energy, playfulness, and a level of sophistication as the defining attributes of the new brand's character.

JINXING THE PROCESS

The exisiting cat icon sent designers delving into the folklore of the black cat, uncovering hundreds upon hundreds of recognizable symbols and metaphors. While exploring the black cat's associations with darkness and nighttime, the designers saw some appropriate connections to low-lit clubs and enjoying nights out with friends. Additionally, the bad luck aspect of the black cat lent an irreverent edge to the brand, an attribute that resonates with the target market. The word "jinx" further suggested the risky, mysterious characteristics of a black cat. Dossier also saw an advantage to developing a new descriptor to strengthen its product

■ Targeting the twenty-something nightclub scene, the Sour Puss liqueur brand expanded into a new category when it introduced a ready-to-drink (RTD) beverage.

DESIGN FIRM
DOSSIER CREATIVE, INC.

CREATIVE DIRECTOR
DON CHISHOLM

DESIGNER
PATRICK SMITH

CLIENT
PHILLIPS DISTILLING

The Jinx mark dominates the beverage carton's panels in a playful way, while the circles allude to both the beverage's carbonation and its bubbly personality. The typography of the Jinx mark dominates the carton's panels, identifying the brand in a playful way.

Dossier explored different visual approaches that addressed both the brand's character and the need for its logo to look different from those of the competition.

- Riffing on Sour Puss' original cat logo and the company name itself, the new icon for the Jinx brand was designed as a silhouette of a sassy cat strutting along an imaginary rooftop created by the stylized letters of the name.

differentiation other than the standard vodka cooler or rum beverage. They defined Jinx with the descriptor, sour citrus, which highlights the drink's key feature: a subtle, sour lemon aftertaste.

CAPTURING THE SLY LOOK

With the name in place, the designers began concepting a look that would express the qualities of the brand. After surveying the existing RTD landscape, they concluded that only a bold, graphic package would catch the attention of its intended audience, so they explored different visual approaches that addressed both the brand's character and the need for its logo to look different from the competition. It was important to capture the appropriate mix of irreverence, fun, and sophistication in an engaging way.

After many experiments with Sour Puss' original cat logo, what evolved into the Jinx icon was a silhouette of a cat strolling along a rooftop. For the carton, Dossier wanted to convey the bar environment that Jinx would be found in by alluding to music, light, and shadow. The typography of the Jinx mark dominates the carton's panels, identifying the brand in a playful way. The use of irregularly sized vertical stripes in vibrant colors conveys a sense of energy and suggests the planes of light found in a darkened room such as a lounge or a dance floor. The color palette is warm and inviting, and the circles allude to both the carbonation of the beverage and its bubbly personality.

Jinx Sour Citrus established itself as an appropriate and natural complement to the endorsing brand, Sour Puss. The new beverage builds a memorable new relationship with the consumer, setting the stage for its long-term success.

Amanda Teillet

6 Station Approach, Penarth
South Glamorgan, CF64 3EE

t 02920 705858
m 07727213284
guiliguili.co.uk

Childrenswear, gifts and toys
From newborn to 6, stocking the latest
designs from Mayoral, Dandelion,
Nonkie's, Uttam Kids, No Added Sugar,
The Next Big Thing Clothing plus fun
accessories, gifts and toys.

■ Playful yet sophisticated, the logo and illustrations for Guili Guili, a retailer of
children's clothes, toys, and gifts, appeals to both children and their parents.

A FUN NAME

Guili Guili is a retailer of children's clothes, toys, and gifts based in Cardiff, Wales. The shops stock exclusive, high-end European children's wear brands and is well known for its vibrantly colorful designs and high-quality toys and gifts. Guili Guili needed an identity that would position it as an innovative, fashion-forward market-leading company and would capture the attention of its target audience.

One of the biggest challenges of this particular naming and identity project was that it needed to reflect the meaning of the company name, but not in a literal way; the name Guili Guili is French for "tickle tickle" (pronounced *gill-eeee gill-eeeee*).

DESIGN FIRM
ELFEN

CREATIVE DIRECTOR
GUTO EVANS

DESIGNER
WAYNE HARRIS

CLIENT
GUILI GUILI

- The name Guili Guili is French for "tickle tickle." Guili Guili needed an identity that would position it as an innovative, fashion-forward market-leading company and would capture the attention of its target audience.

• Elfen recognized that, in addition to developing a logo, using character illustrations would also add value to the brand.

■ The Guili Guili birds are integral elements that appear on all the store's materials.

PLAYING WITH IDENTITY

For Guili Guili to position itself in the high-end retail market, they worked closely with the design agency Elfen to develop a chic yet playful brand. Having previously worked on a number of projects that targeted a similar audience, Elfen recognized that, in addition to developing a logo, using character illustrations would also add value to the brand. After experimenting with different organic forms, Elfen created their own species of bird, the "Guili Guili." Guili Guili seemed like the perfect name for a bird and it was easy to imagine it trilling the "guili guili" sound. They envisioned the bird as a colorful, playful character perfect for children, especially with its giggle-inducing name. This, in turn, informed the logo itself—a kid-friendly typeface framed by an organic shape.

The client was delighted with the logo and illustrations because they proved to be popular with children while also appealing to parents. An important part of this brand's personality is the Guili Guili bird, which appears on all corporate materials including business cards, flyers, and shop exteriors.

■ These three dated renderings show the progression of designs for the Hangar 18 logo, with the 2005 version the one currently being used. The original 1998 logo was redesigned in 2003, creating a new wordmark and the H18 icon.

THE INSPIRATION IS OUT THERE

Hangar 18 Creative Group was founded in Vancouver in 1996. At the time, graphic designer Sean Carter had a one-person design consultancy while art director Vida Jurcic and copywriter Nigel Yonge had been working as a freelance advertising creative team. Because both enterprises had neighboring offices on the seventh floor of the same office building, they got to know each other fairly well. One day,

between computer pinball games, the teams discussed merging into an advertising and design company. With a clink of three beers at the now-defunct Vancouver Hard Rock Café, a company was born and they landed their very first creative assignment: naming themselves.

During that time, the TV show, *The X Files*, was being regularly shot on location around Vancouver. One night, a

DESIGN FIRM
HANGAR 18 CREATIVE GROUP

CREATIVE DIRECTORS
SEAN CARTER, VIDA JURCIC, NIGEL YONGE

DESIGNERS
SEAN CARTER, VIDA JURCIC, NIGEL YONGE

CLIENT
HANGAR 18 CREATIVE GROUP

• Although in the business of creating corporate identities, the most difficult logo for a designer to create is the one for his own company.

■ U.S. Air Force hangar number 18 is supposedly where the spaceship and alien bodies from the infamous Roswell crash site were stored. The team had a lot of fun creating UFO-themed marketing tools such as abduc-tee shirts.

scene was being filmed on the street below their office that required a man operating a massive floodlight in a cherry picker to be stationed 100 feet up, right outside their seventh-story office windows. The three struck up a conversation with the man on the cherry picker, who explained he was filming a scene about Area 51—the parcel of U.S. military-controlled Nevada land that is purported to house alien technology. The creatives were intrigued and further researched the alien theme, deciding to name their company Hangar 18 after the U.S. Air Force hangar where spaceship wreckage and alien bodies were supposedly stored after the so-called Roswell incident of 1947.

Following through on the alien-themed name, Hangar 18 developed spaceship-shaped Frisbees, abduc-tee shirts, and other UFO-themed self-promotions. And while the look evolved as the company grew larger, the fun-loving, beer-clinking Hangar 18 brand endures.

IDENTITY FROM THE UNKNOWN

Although in the business of creating corporate identities, the most difficult logo for any designer to create is the one for his own company. Knowing this, Hangar 18, decided to put its logo's fate in supernatural hands. One night, over beer and sushi, they brought out a Ouija board, dimmed the lights and channeled Pheezborg, the patron saint of entrepreneurial graphic designers. When asked what typeface they should use, the board repeatedly spelled out T-e-m-p-l-a-t-e G-o-t-h-i-c E-x-p-a-n-d-e-d. The shape of the logo was dictated when the planchette simply moved in an oval pattern. Three more clinks of beers and the company's destiny was set.

The firm's name was inspired by the TV show, *The X Files*, which was shot at locations around Vancouver.

Contributors

3
8220 La Mirada NE, Suite 500
Albuquerque, NM 87109
USA
T. 505.293.2333
F. 505.293.1198
www.whois3.com
Page 174

BAMBOO
503-119 N 4th Street
Minneapolis, MN 55401
USA
T. 612.332.7105
F. 612.332.7101
www.bamboo-design.com
Page 138

BLU CONCEPT INC.
103-1104 Hornby Street
Vancouver, BC V6Z 1V8
Canada
T. 604.872.2583
F. 604.872.2588
www.bluconcept.com
Page 136

BRAVE NEW WORLD
The Textile Centre, 1 Kenwyn Street
Parnell, Auckland
New Zealand
T. 64.9.358.2448
F. 64.9.358.2447
www.bravenewworld.co.nz
Page 22, 38

CHEN DESIGN
331 Camarillo Street, Apt. D
Placentia, CA 92870
USA
T. 714.223.6997
F. 714.278.2390
Page 80

DESIGN RANCH
809 West 17th Street
Kansas City, MO 64108
USA
T. 816.472.8668
F. 816.472.8778
www.design-ranch.com
Page 130

DEW GIBBONS
49 Tabernacle Street
London, England EC2A 4AA
United Kingdom
T. 44.0.20.7689.8999
F. 44.0.20.7689.9377
www.dewgibbons.com
Page 100

DOSSIER CREATIVE, INC.
402-611 Alexander Street
Vancouver, BC V6A 1E1
Canada
T. 604.255.2077
F. 604.255.2097
www.dossiercreative.com
Page 26, 178

ELFEN
20 Harrowby Lane, Cardiff Bay
Cardiff, South Glamorgan, Wales CF10 5GN
United Kingdom
T. 44.292.048.4824
F. 44.292.048.4823
www.elfen.co.uk
Page 182

EXHIBIT A: DESIGN GROUP
2-25 East Sixth Avenue
Vancouver, BC V5T 1J3
Canada
T. 604.873.1583
F. 604.873.1584
www.exhibitadesigngroup.com
Page 50

FLAT
391 Broadway, 3rd Floor
New York, NY 10013
USA
T. 646.613.8833
F. 646.613.8836
www.flat.com
Page 84

FROST DESIGN
15 Foster Street
Surry Hills, Sydney NSW 2010
Australia
T. 61.2.9280.4233
F. 61.2.9280.4266
www.frostdesign.com.au
Page 62

FUTUREBRAND JAPAN
23F. 1-4-28 Mita Minato-Ku
Tokyo 108-0073
Japan
T. 81.0.3.5418.1821
F. 81.0.3.5418.1822
www.futurebrand.com
Page 30

FUTUREBRAND SINGAPORE
371 Beach Road
#04 - 04 Keypoint
Singapore 199957
T. 65.6238.3868
F. 65.6738.3018
www.futurebrand.com
Page 56

GIOTTO DESIGN
Juan González N35-135 edf. Metropoli of. 606
Quito, Ecuador
South America
T. 593.2.2461075
F. 593.2.2461075
www.giottodesign.net
Page 154

ZINKIA ENTERTAINMENT
Infantas 27, Planta 1
Madrid 28004
Spain
T. 91.524.03.65
F. 91.524.07.37
www.zinkia.com
Page 168

GREY WORLDWIDE
1000-850 West Hastings Street
Vancouver, BC V6C 1E1
Canada
T. 604.687.1001
F. 604.682.1827
www.grey.net
Page 46

H2D2
Kaiser STR. 79
60329 Frankfurt
Germany
T. 49.69.904.304.84
F. 49.69.904.304.86
www.h2d2.de
Page 64

HANGAR 18 CREATIVE GROUP
220-1737 West 3rd Avenue
Vancouver, BC V6J 1K7
Canada
T. 604.737.7111
F. 604.737.7166
www.hangar18creative.com
Page 186

HORNALL ANDERSON DESIGN WORKS
1300-710 Second Avenue
Seattle, WA 98104
USA
T. 206.467.5800
F. 206.167.6411
www.hadw.com
Page 92, 140

JAMES BATES/ATOM
202 Kensington Church St.
London, England W8 4DP
United Kingdom
T. 44.0.20.7229.5720
F. 44.0.20.7229.5721
www.atomweb.net
Page 128

KARAKTER
3rd Floor, 14-18 Old Street
London, England EC1V 9BH
United Kingdom
T. 44.20.7553.9020
F. 44.20.7253.9020
www.karakter.co.uk
Page 72

KARACTERS DESIGN GROUP
1600-777 Hornby Street
Vancouver, BC V6Z 2T3
Canada
T. 604.640.4327
F. 604.608.4452
www.karacters.com
Page 40, 148

LAYFIELD
Level 3, 230 Clarence Street
Sydney NSW 2000
Australia
T. 61.2.9269.0789
F. 61.2.9264.7264
www.stephenlayfield.com
Page 36, 110

LISKA + ASSOCIATES
515 N. State Street, 23rd Floor
Chicago, IL 60610
USA
T. 312.644.4400
F. 312.644.9650
www.liska.com
Page 156

MORTENSEN DESIGN, INC.
416 Bush Street
Mountain View, CA 94041
USA
T. 650.988.0946
F. 650.988.0926
www.mortdes.com
Page 86

PEARLFISHER
50 Brook Green
London, England W6 7BJ,
United Kingdom
T. 44.0.20.7603.8666
F. 44.0.20.7605.1888
www.pearlfisher.com
Page 116, 118

PENTAGRAM DESIGN
Leibnizstrasse 60
Berlin 10629
Germany
T. 49.30.2787.610
F. 49.30.2787.6110
www.pentagram.de
Page 126

RETHINK
200-1425 West Pender Street
Vancouver, BC V6G 2S3
Canada
T. 604.685.8911
F. 604.685.9004
www.rethinkadvertising.com
Page 68, 76

SALTERBAXTER
202 Kensington Church Street
London, England W8 4DP
United Kingdom
T. 44.0.20.7229.5720
F. 44.0.20.7229.5721
www.salterbaxter.com
Page 152

SEA
70 St. John Street
London, England EC1M 4DT
United Kingdom
T. 44.20.7566.3100
F. 44.20.7566.3101
www.seadesign.co.uk
Page 96, 160

SOULSIGHT
P° Castellana n° 173 3°
Madrid 28046
Spain
T. 34.91.571.8609
F. 34.91.572.3167
www.soul-sight.com
Page 82

WOW BRANDING
101-1300 Richards Street
Vancouver, BC V6B 3G6
Canada
T. 604.683.5655
F. 866.877.4032
www.wowbranding.com
Page 104, 120

About WOW Branding

WOW Branding is a seriously innovative brand-development company based in Vancouver, Canada.

Our core purpose is helping our clients bring their entrepreneurial vision to life. Through our twelve years of experience we have learned that our clients fall into two categories: companies that need to launch with a new name, identity, and a compelling brand story; and established companies that need to revitalize their brand due to loss of clarity and focus both internally and externally.

Our methodologies help challenge our clients to define who they are and how they are positioned, in order to create an authentic brand identity that all stakeholders can be proud of.

www.wowbranding.com